Dedicated to the thirtieth anniversary of the independence of Ukraine and published with the assistance of the Ministry of Culture and Information Policy of Ukraine and the Ukrainian Book Institute.

Published in the UK by Scholastic, 2023
1 London Bridge, London, SE1 9BG
Scholastic Ireland, 89E Lagan Road, Dublin Industrial Estate, Glasnevin, Dublin, D11 HP5F

SCHOLASTIC and associated logos are trademarks and/or registered trademarks of Scholastic Inc.

First published in Ukraine by My Bookshelf Publishing House, 2021

Text © Inna Kovalyshena, 2023
Illustrations © Galochka Ch, 2023
Translated by Hanna Leliv

ISBN 978 07023 2493 2

A CIP catalogue record for this book is available from the British Library.

All rights reserved.
This book is sold subject to the condition that it shall not, by way of trade or otherwise, be lent, hired out or otherwise circulated in any form of binding or cover other than that in which it is published. No part of this publication may be reproduced, stored in a retrieval system, or transmitted in any form or by any other means (electronic, mechanical, photocopying, recording or otherwise) without prior written permission of Scholastic Limited.

Printed by C& C in China.
Paper made from wood grown in sustainable forests and other controlled sources.

1 3 5 7 9 10 8 6 4 2

www.scholastic.co.uk

A COOL HISTORY OF UKRAINE

FROM DINOSAURS ---→ TILL NOW

WRITTEN BY
INNA KOVALYSHENA

ILLUSTRATED BY
GALOCHKA CH

Translated from the Ukrainian by Hanna Leliv

■SCHOLASTIC

CONTENTS

1. CHALK, ICE AND BONES 
2. WHAT KIND OF PEOPLE WERE THEY? 
3. THE GREEKS AND PEOPLE THEY WROTE ABOUT
9. PARENTS AND CHILDREN OF THE FIRST UKRAINIAN WAR OF INDEPENDENCE
8. TO REMEMBER WHO YOU ARE AND SURVIVE
10. ATTEMPTS TO TURN THE TIDE
11. HANDING OVER THE FLAG

1 CHALK, ICE AND BONES

Dmytryk saw his friends from afar – they'd gathered by the secret cliff. There it was: Aliye's black hair, Sashko's tuft of red hair and Yasia's chestnut plaits with purple strands. His three friends were peering at something in the grass.

"You're late," Sashko grumbled.

Dmytryk whipped out his phone: "Mama called."

His mother fought in the 57th Motorized Infantry Brigade in the east of Ukraine, and you never knew when she would get another chance to call her loved ones.

His friends nodded. Mama was a good enough reason to be late.

"Look what we've found on the lake shore," Yasia said, gesturing toward the grass. "Do you know what that might be?"

Dmytryk looked at two rocks.

"My grandpa called them devil's fingers," he said, pointing at the longish one.

"And my grandma said they were the heads of lightning arrows. But I guess they're neither."

Aliye ran her fingers along their find thoughtfully.

"I think I know who can tell us about them," she said.

Back at the holiday camp, Aliye shouted:

"Da-a-a-dy!"

"What happened, *kızım* (meaning 'my daughter' in Crimean Tatar)?" a man with glasses said, looking out of a pavilion in the park.

"Do you know what these are?" Aliye dashed to the pavilion like an arrow. Her friends tagged along.

"I do," her father nodded. "These are mollusc fossils."

"Fossils?" Sashko said, perking up. "From the dinosaur era? Perhaps these are fossils of dinosaurs, not molluscs, Mister Rustem?"

"But what kind of dinosaurs lived here?" Yasia cut him short.

"Textbooks don't mention specific species!" Dmytryk said, getting excited.

"Alright," Rustem said, interrupting them. "I'll tell you the whole story. Come on over here, sit down.

"Dinosaurs appeared on our planet 235 million years ago, in the Triassic period. Only one continent existed on Earth back then. It was called Pangea. It was surrounded by an ocean called Panthalassa. It was warmer on our planet than it is now. Many parts of Pangea received very little rain. That was the time of archosaurs, a group of reptiles that included not just dinosaurs, but ancient crocodiles and turtles.

The first turtles, dinosaurs and mammals appeared. And there were belemnites swimming in the seas. Those molluscs looked like squids, and these oblong rocks are belemnite fossils."

"But we are in the Cherkasy region, which is in the middle of Ukraine," Sashko said, frowning. "How would marine creatures end up here?"

Rustem laughed.

"Of course, the sea is far away now. But it wasn't always like that. In the Triassic period, there was only one continent, so much of what is now land was under the sea. And in the Jurassic era, the next period that started about 201 million years

ago, Pangea split apart to form two continents: Laurasia and Gondwana. New oceans appeared, such as the Atlantic. It was during the Jurassic period that the first birds and early mammals appeared, and **ammonites** lived in the ocean and seas. It was **a kind of squid mixed with a snail**."

The children giggled.

"The Jurassic period was followed by the Cretaceous period, roughly **145 million years ago**. Back then, all of Ukraine apart from Crimea, Donbas and the Carpathians was the ocean floor."

"And what about dinosaurs?" Dmytryk asked. "The Jurassic period was the dinosaur era, for sure."

"Only two species have been found in Ukraine. Both in Crimea. Only one of them could be identified. It was a herbivore called Riabininohadros."

"Never heard of it," Sashko declared in the sceptical tone of a dinosaur expert.

"It's a close relative of Iguanodon."

"Well, if you say so…" Sashko said thoughtfully and pulled up a browser on his smartphone to check out those Iguanodons.

"And who lived in the water? I mean apart from those … belemnites and ammonites?" Aliye spoke up.

"Oh, many different creatures at different times. Huge rays and sharks. Also, plesiosaurs and mosasaurs – giant marine reptiles. Sea crocodiles."

"Why did they die out?" Yasia wondered.

"Because **a meteorite fell on Earth**," Sashko explained.

"It's just one of the hypotheses," Rustem said. "According to another one, the species died out during the Cretaceous period as a result of **earthquakes and volcanic eruptions**. Another less popular theory blames **flowering plants**: they spread across the planet,

RIABININOHADROS WEBERAE

displacing conifers and ferns. The herbivorous dinosaurs couldn't eat them and died out. And then the predators that hunted those herbivores died out, too."

"Oh, I see ... and what happened after the dinosaurs died out?" Yasia wondered.

"The Cenozoic era began. The continents started to look similar to the ones we have now. The entire south of Ukraine was the large, shallow Paratethys Sea, home to fish, turtles and salamanders. Ancient sea birds nested on its shores. Their fossils are often found in the Luhansk region. The Paratethys Sea dried up and then filled with water again several times until it vanished six million years ago, leaving behind the **Aral**

HARE

DASORNIS

and Caspian Lakes, as well as the **Black Sea Lake,** which later became the **Black Sea**.

"The planet became much colder. Ice ages occurred from time to time, bringing freezing temperatures. Huge glaciers on the poles spread much further than now – up to the borders of Ukraine. There were five ice ages in total."

"So, that's when mammoths lived in Ukraine?" Aliye asked.

"Exactly. And not only them. Cave bears, lions, hyenas, woolly rhinos, as well as hamsters, hares and various birds lived here, too."

"Why did they all die out? Because it grew warmer?"

"There are many theories. Some say that people hunted them, others blame the warming. I prefer a new version: **the entire ecosystem was built around the mammoths, so when they vanished, everything else disappeared, too. And the mammoths were wiped out by an epidemic**."

"And what happened afterward?"

"The world became quite similar to the one we know now. Except that saiga antelopes and wild goats lived in the forests." (These were two of numerous extinct species.)

"I'm wondering when humans appeared here," Yasia said, turning the ammonite over and over in her hands. "It's millions of years that we're talking about. The continents changed shape. The seas dried up or formed. Did it all happen without humans?"

"I don't study humans," Rustem said, and shrugged. "But we are a very young species, indeed. As far as I remember, the earliest members of the genus Homo (the earliest human-like creatures) originated in Africa about 2.4 million years ago. Researchers call them Homo habilis. And Homo sapiens, to which all modern humans belong, appeared **around 300,000 years ago**. They reached the Ukrainian lands even

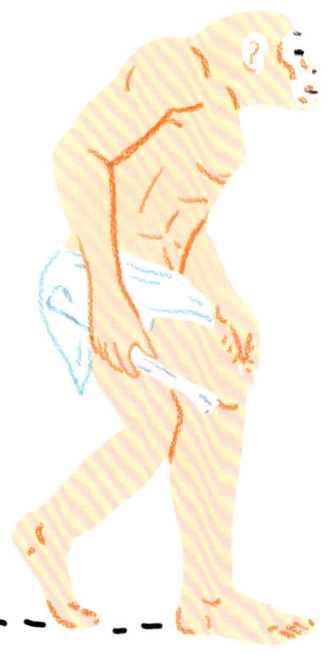

HOMO HABILIS

AFRICA

later ... well, I'm sure your history teachers will tell you all about it."

The children looked at one another. Aliye and Dmytryk, who had just finished the fifth grade, mumbled:

"Oh yeah. Teachers will tell us, for sure."

"I have an idea!" Yasia exclaimed. "Let's do some research and write our own history book! A fascinating one, not another boring textbook."

"Let's create a page on social media instead!" Dmytryk said, picking up on her idea. "It's easier, and its followers would be able to add info. We can even make a game. A quest! The page could be called 'A Cool History of Ukraine'!"

"Sounds interesting, guys, but we all go back to our hometowns in a week," Sashko said, sceptical as always. "You won't travel that often from Zaporizhzhia to Kropyvnytskyi, let alone to Ivano-Frankivsk or Chernihiv."

"We can meet online. Our parents will help us." Aliye turned to Rustem. "Won't you?"

"Of course," Rustem said, hugging his daughter.

HOMO SAPIENS

UKRAINE

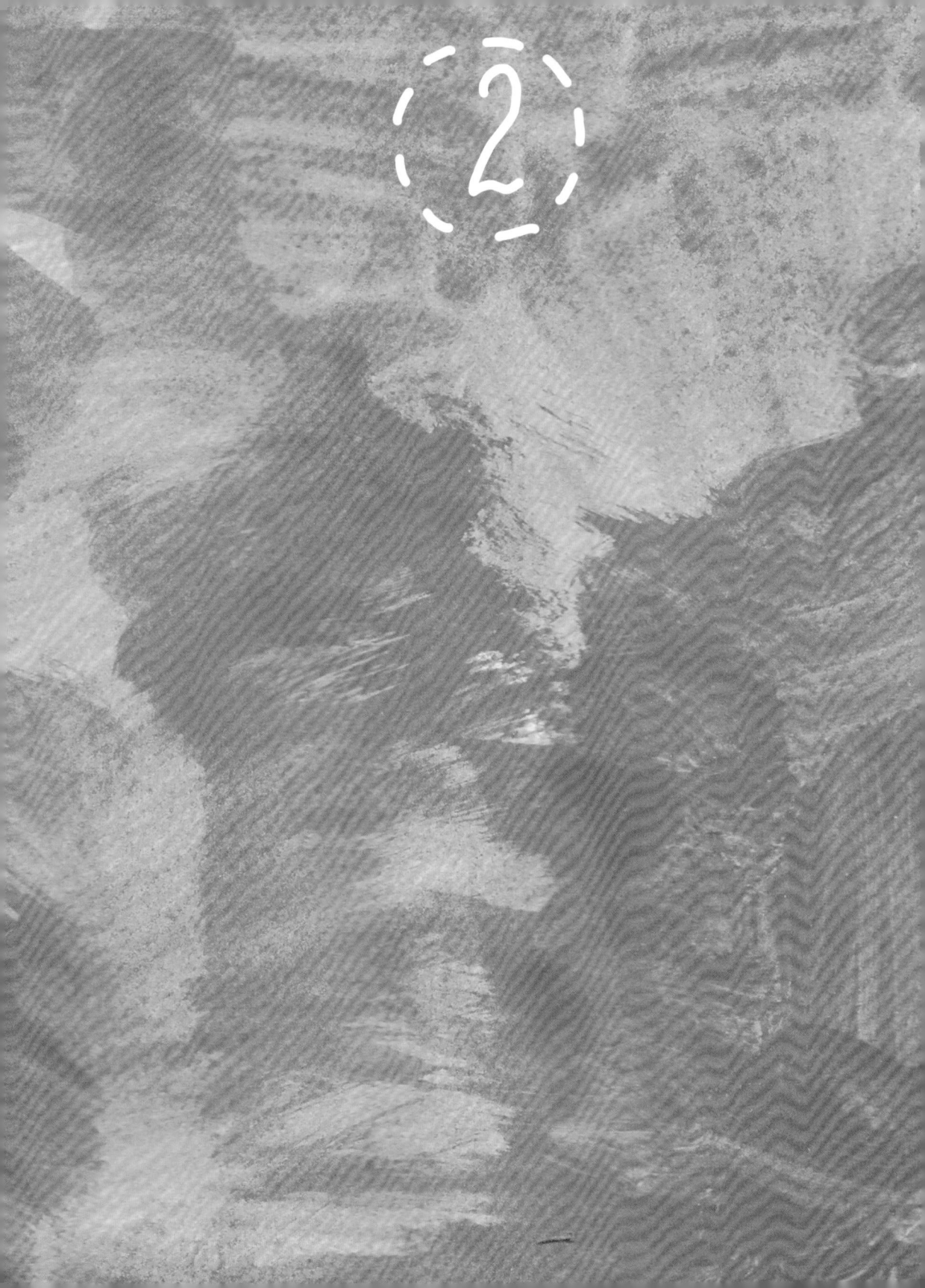

2 WHAT KIND OF PEOPLE WERE THEY?

BUT I DON'T THINK YOUR FRIENDS WILL REMEMBER YOUR ARRANGEMENT

Yasia was worried that her new friends would forget about the quest as soon as they arrived home. Her parents also doubted Yasia's friends would remember:

"I can take you to the museum, of course, if you want to," her father said. "But I don't think your friends will remember your arrangement."

"They will!" Yasia said, stomping her foot. She couldn't tell who she was trying harder to convince – her parents or herself.

School was starting soon – what if her friends just gave up on their idea? They would have lessons. Homework. Other things to do.

But Dmytryk's text message – "When are we meeting? You won't believe what I found!" – eased Yasia's worries. They met online the next evening.

"So, what did you find out?" Aliye asked, shooing her cat away from the keyboard.

"It turns out that two species of

THEY WILL!

humans used to live here in Ukraine! It was about 40,000 years ago, in the period called the Paleolithic! There were more species around the world, but we had only two – Homo sapiens and Neanderthals."

"How did they differ?"

Dmytryk looked serious.

"Here, I found a comparison chart talking about the differences between the two species."

"Neanderthals **invented rope**. I mean they were the first to twist the fibers together into a thread or rope like we still do now. And they also **made the world's oldest flute**,

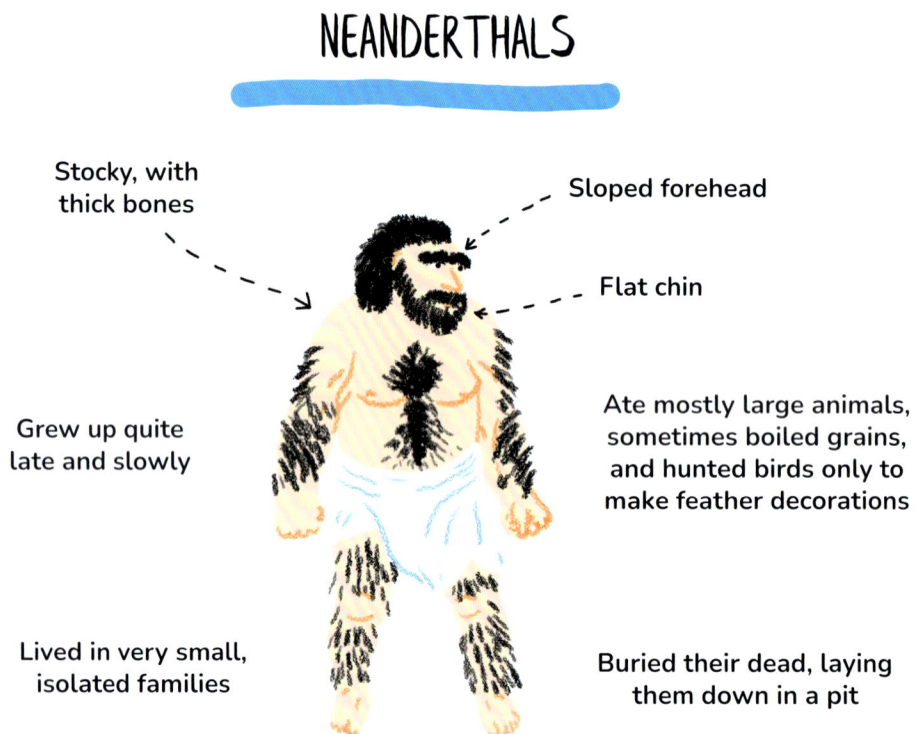

NEANDERTHALS

- Stocky, with thick bones
- Sloped forehead
- Flat chin
- Grew up quite late and slowly
- Ate mostly large animals, sometimes boiled grains, and hunted birds only to make feather decorations
- Lived in very small, isolated families
- Buried their dead, laying them down in a pit

Native inhabitants of Europe

which means they made music. And they **had their own language**, too! When our ancestors – early modern humans – came to Europe, they adopted Neanderthal methods for making rope and stone tools. And Neanderthals adopted practices from early modern humans, in turn."

"And where are Neanderthals now?" Aliye asked suspiciously. "Did they also die out?"

Dmytryk nodded, and Sashko said:

"Homo sapiens killed them. They organized some kind of a war and just killed them."

"No, it's not true!" Dmytryk

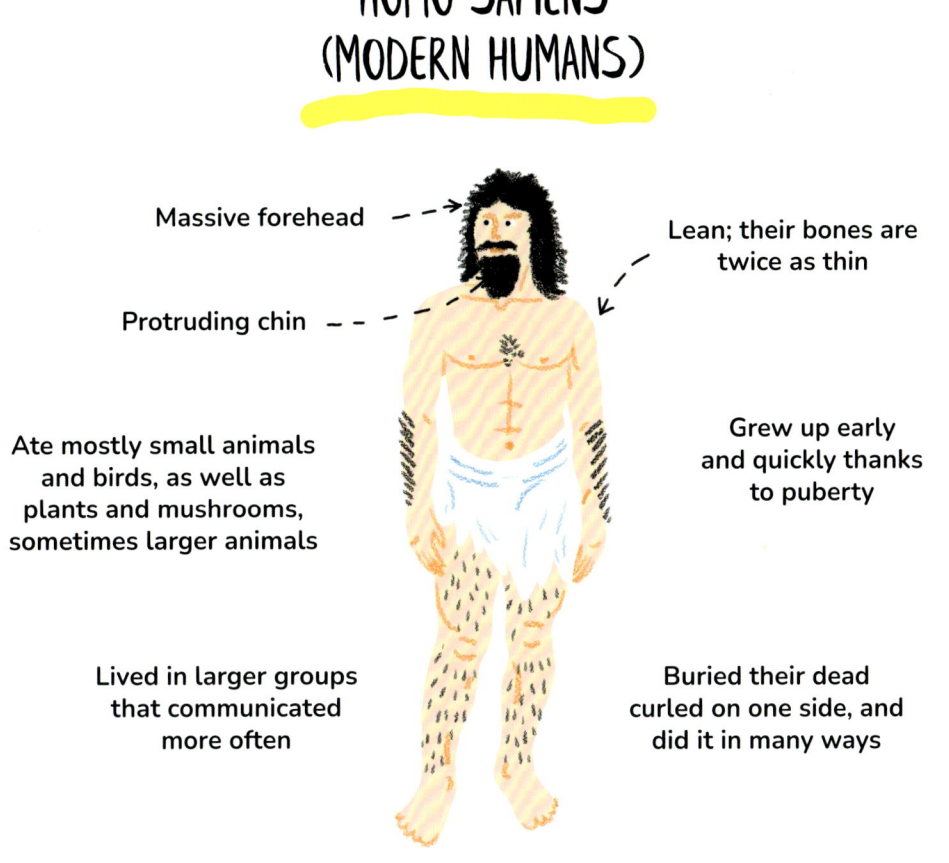

HOMO SAPIENS (MODERN HUMANS)

- Massive forehead
- Protruding chin
- Lean; their bones are twice as thin
- Ate mostly small animals and birds, as well as plants and mushrooms, sometimes larger animals
- Grew up early and quickly thanks to puberty
- Lived in larger groups that communicated more often
- Buried their dead curled on one side, and did it in many ways

Came to Europe from Africa

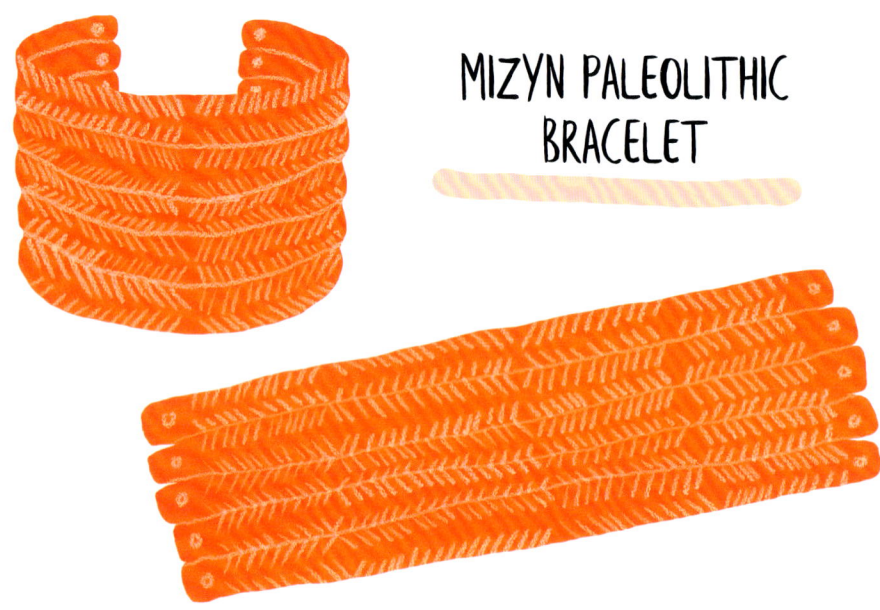

MIZYN PALEOLITHIC BRACELET

protested. "Neanderthals were stronger – and as smart as our ancestors. They were also used to a cold climate. Had there been a war, they would've killed us alright. But we co-existed together. In fact, Neanderthals may have started to die out even before our ancestors arrived in Europe."

"So what? None of them survived?" Yasia asked, her voice sad.

"They had children with Homo sapiens, and those children had children. **Today, most people have some Neanderthal DNA**. But yes, 40,000 years ago, our ancestors were all alone in Europe. They hunted mammoths, bisons and horses and followed them as they moved. Small animals were also their prey. They picked edible plants, made art and tamed dogs. **And they built shelters from animal skins and bones**."

"Why did they do that?"

"Well, during the Ice Age, it was tundra here – a vast polar steppe, with very few trees."

"Oh yes," Yasia nodded. "I saw shelters like that in the museum. There was the Mizyn Paleolithic site in the **Chernihiv region**. And the Mezhyrich site in the **Cherkasy region**."

"Did those people become homeless after the mammoths died out?" Sashko asked.

"No, they looked for other ways to live," Aliye said. "They **started to make more complex tools**. A bit later, there was the **Neolithic Revolution,** about 12,000 years ago. The Neolithic Revolution was a period when people learned to grow plants, domesticated animals, settled down, and **started to make things from clay, weave materials and smelt copper**. It was

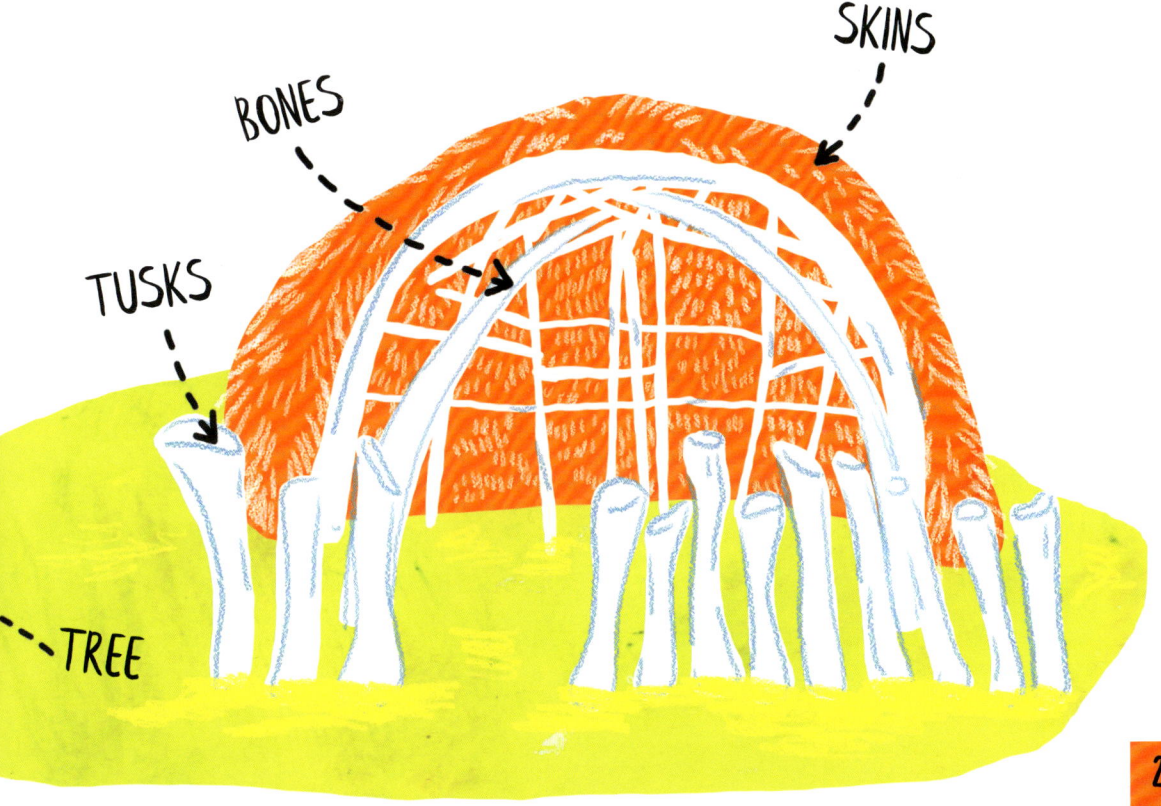

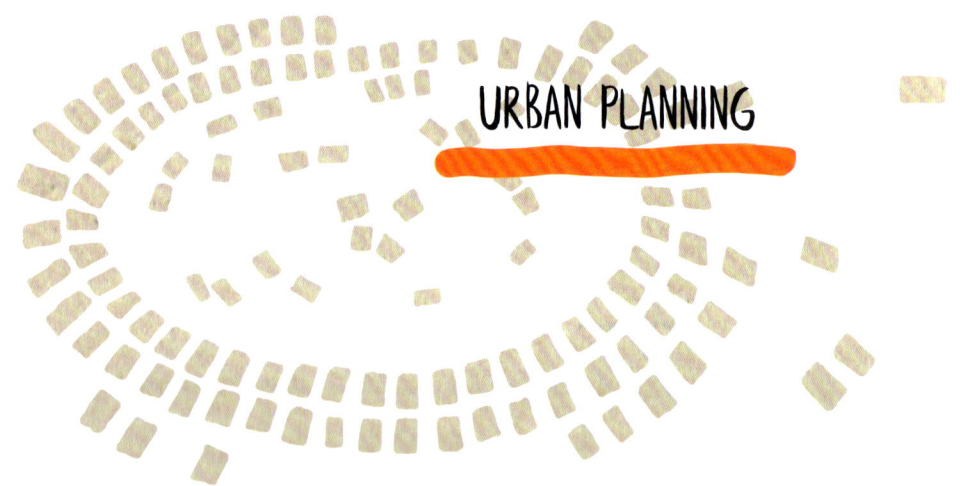

URBAN PLANNING

an incredible breakthrough: **people no longer searched for food in the wild but grew it by themselves**. That's why it's called a revolution. It's sometimes also known as the Agricultural Revoluion."

"Right!" Yasia said, jumping in. "My parents took me to a **museum in Lehedzyno**. They told us about the Trypillyan culture. Those people lived in Ukraine around 7,000 years ago. They built wonderful villages with **huts laid out in circles**. The largest village was Talianky – 15,000 people lived there! It was the largest settlement in Europe at that point."

"Perhaps it was not a village but a city?"

"No, they didn't have any cities. In a city, people would do crafts and trade, whereas the Trypillyans were mostly farmers, though they did have some craftsmen. Look at this. That's why **their settlements are often called proto-cities**."

"And what was the name of their country?" Sashko wondered.

"They didn't have a country at the time. They **lived in large families**, and the **families united into tribes**. A few tribes might have lived in one proto-city but we don't know

it for a fact. Still, they did not have counties like we have today – with taxes, money and rulers. There was no written language, either, so we have no idea what they called themselves."

"What about their neighbours? Perhaps they wrote something about the Trypillyans?" Aliye asked.

"There was no written language in the whole world back then," Sashko said with a serious look. "It was invented in the Middle East later, in the Bronze Age, around **3,400 BCE**. It's called the Bronze Age because at that time, **people had discovered how to alloy copper with tin and get a new kind of metal – bronze**."

"And what did the Trypillyans do in the Bronze Age?"

"Nothing," Sashko grumbled. "The Trypillyan culture did not exist anymore. There was Yamna or Pit Grave culture. And the Corded Ware culture. And many other cultures that existed all at the same time or later."

"Why did the Trypillyans disappear, by the way?" Dmytryk wondered.

"Other catastrophes happened," Sashko said with a sigh. "Drought, cooling, epidemics. The Trypillyans abandoned their proto-cities and became nomads in the south of what is now Ukraine, and then they just vanished. They probably passed on a handful of genes to the inhabitants of present-day Podillia, but it's not an established fact."

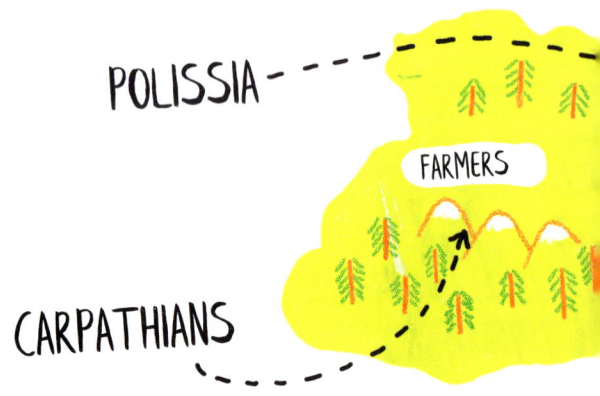

"It's a shame," Aliye said wistfully. "They did so many nice things ... And what about the cultures you just mentioned? What did those people do?"

"It depends. Some of them were herders and roamed through the steppe with their livestock. They were the first in the history of humankind **to tame horses**. Others were farmers in the forest steppe, the Polissia region and the Carpathian Mountains. **Copper mines** already existed in Donbas at that point, but there wasn't that much bronze as Ukraine did not have tin deposits."

"Are you saying that Ukrainian metallurgy is 3,000 years old?" Aliye said, smiling.

"More like **4,000**, at the very least," Sashko said.

"But still, it's a shame they did not invent written language and leave some records about their life," Dmytro said sadly. "By the way, do we have any records about anyone else?"

3 THE GREEKS AND PEOPLE THEY WROTE ABOUT

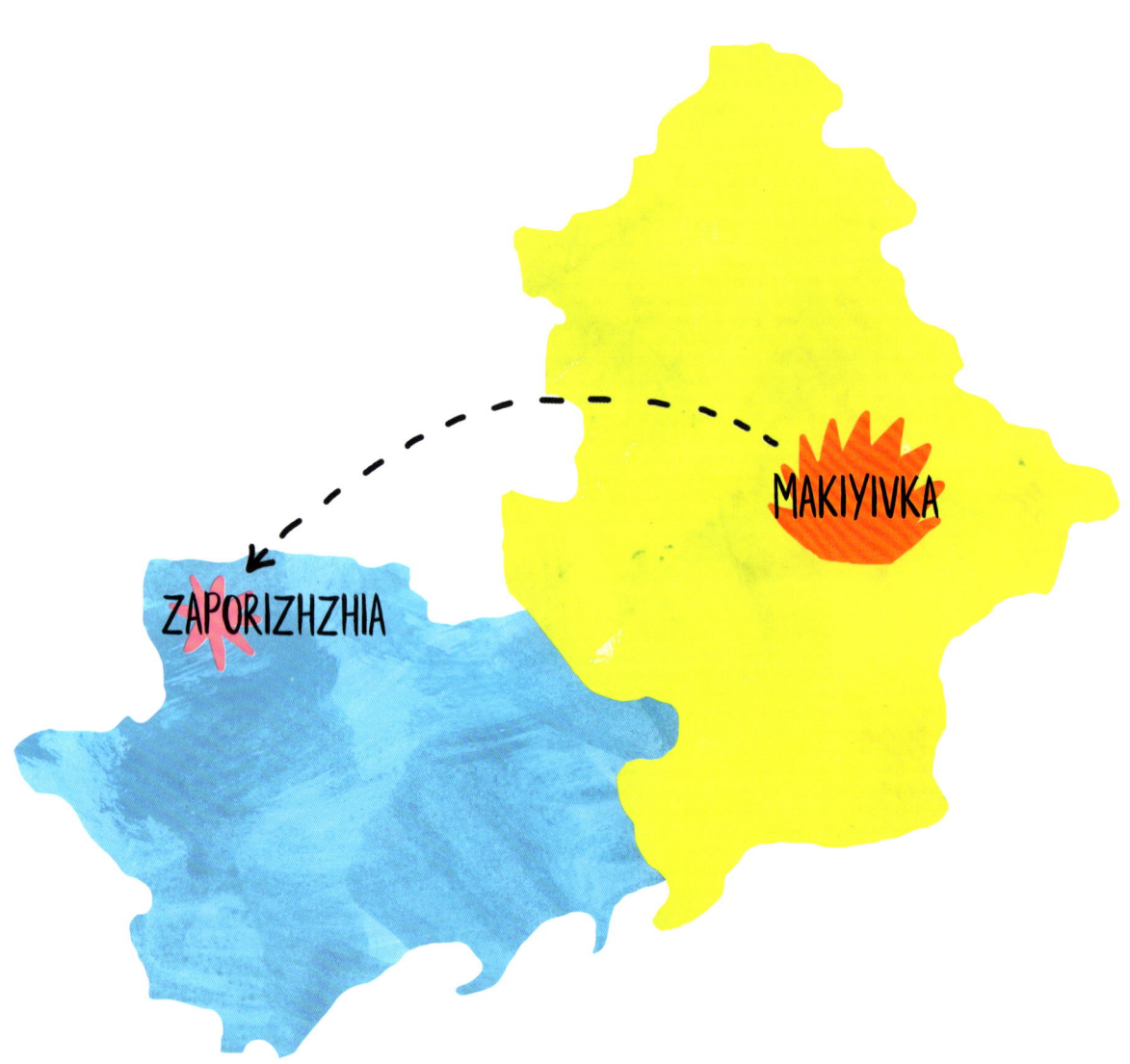

"I'm so glad to hear that you're interested in history!" Sashko's mother said the next day. "I hope you'll share what you learn with me. I hated history lessons in school. Our teacher was a bore, and all he did was demand that we memorize dates. It was also thought that those days were long gone and didn't mean anything anymore. But now that the war has come, it turns out they mean a lot."

Sashko already wished he hadn't asked his mother for help. She knew nothing about the Iron Age that came after the Bronze Age. He didn't mean to remind her of the war, either. But then how can you forget about it if it's all around you? It was the war that forced them to move from Makiyivka to Zaporizhzhia. Sashko thought his new town was just fine. He didn't remember Makiyivka that well, anyway. **It's one thing to move to another town, but it's completely different to leave your home behind without any hope of ever coming back because the enemy has occupied it.**

The next day, it turned out that his mother had managed to drop in to the library in between her two jobs and brought a few books back for him. Frankly, the writing was boring, but Sashko hugged his mother, went to Google, and started to wade through the tangled quotes of Herodotus, **an ancient historian who wrote about Ukraine back when Ukraine did not even exist**.

"How are things going with you?" Yasia asked everyone when they met online again. "I haven't found much here in Chernihiv."

"I found some records about the south of Ukraine and Crimea," Aliye said proudly. "**The arrivals from Ancient Greece built the first cities there back in the seventh century** BCE. They had developed written language by that point and described their own lives and the lives of their new neighbours, the *Cimmerians*, nomads who lived here between the eighth and seventh centuries BCE."

"Right!" Sashko exclaimed. "And the Scythians overthrew the Cimmerians. The Greek historian Herodotus even visited **their country**, *Great Scythia*.

"**Scythians were nomads**, too, but ancient Slavs who were farmers paid tribute to them. Ancient Greeks, also subjects of Great Scythia, called them *Scythian tillers*. Despite being nomads, the Scythians had a complex culture. Royal Scythians ruled the country, some were farmers and others served in the Scythian army, defending their people from attacks. In 513 BCE, the Scythians defeated the army of the Persian Empire, the most powerful empire back in the day. Herodotus wrote that the Persian king Darius I wanted to annex Scythia, making it part of his vast empire. Natural resources were not the only reason. Another one was that Cyrus the Great, the founder of the empire, was defeated by Tomyris, queen of the Massagetae, a Scythian tribe. Darius I dreamed of conquering the Scythians, the greatest warriors of the time. Then he would have surpassed Cyrus's glory.

"However, Darius I lost to three Scythian rulers headed by King Idanthyrsus: Darius's troops passed through Scythia without finding the enemy. The Persians struggled from the lack of food and water, though, and during the nighttime, small Scythian units attacked the Persians,

wreaking havoc, and disappeared into the steppe. In the end, Darius I returned to Persia empty-handed."

"Scythians fought not only with Persians," Aliye said. "They also had enough time to fight with the predecessors of the Greek Empire."

"But the Scythians were much more active in trade," Dmytryk said, jumping in. "They bought wine, olive

SCYTHIAN GOLD COMB

oil, fabrics and all kinds of precious things from the Greeks. And they sold cattle, skins and various things made of them, like horse harnesses, and captured slaves."

"Slaves?" Aliye asked, frowning.

"**Slavery was common back then**. And even when people finally understood that it was bad – which happened not so long ago – they didn't hurry to abolish it," Sashko said, and switched topics. "But the Scythians not only bought precious things from the Greeks – they were skillful jewelers, too! Look at these amazing things they made!

"They also **built huge burial mounds for their dead rulers**. This jewelry and many other fascinating objects were found there. **They put stone idols on top of the mounds**.

"Most of the things we know about the Scythians come from the excavations of grave sites and from Herodotus's writings. For example, he wrote that **a Scythian boy was considered a grown-up man only after he had killed his first enemy in war and taken his scalp**."

"And how do the Greeks fit into this history?" Yasia wondered. "Did they sail here to trade with Scythians? Or Cimmerians?"

"They settled here and traded with other locals," Sashko said. "There are lots of mountains in Greece and not as much fertile soil, so many young men and women from Greek towns boarded ships and sailed to faraway lands. They founded new towns there and grew crops, which they later sold to Greek merchants. **They established**

SCYTHIAN RULER

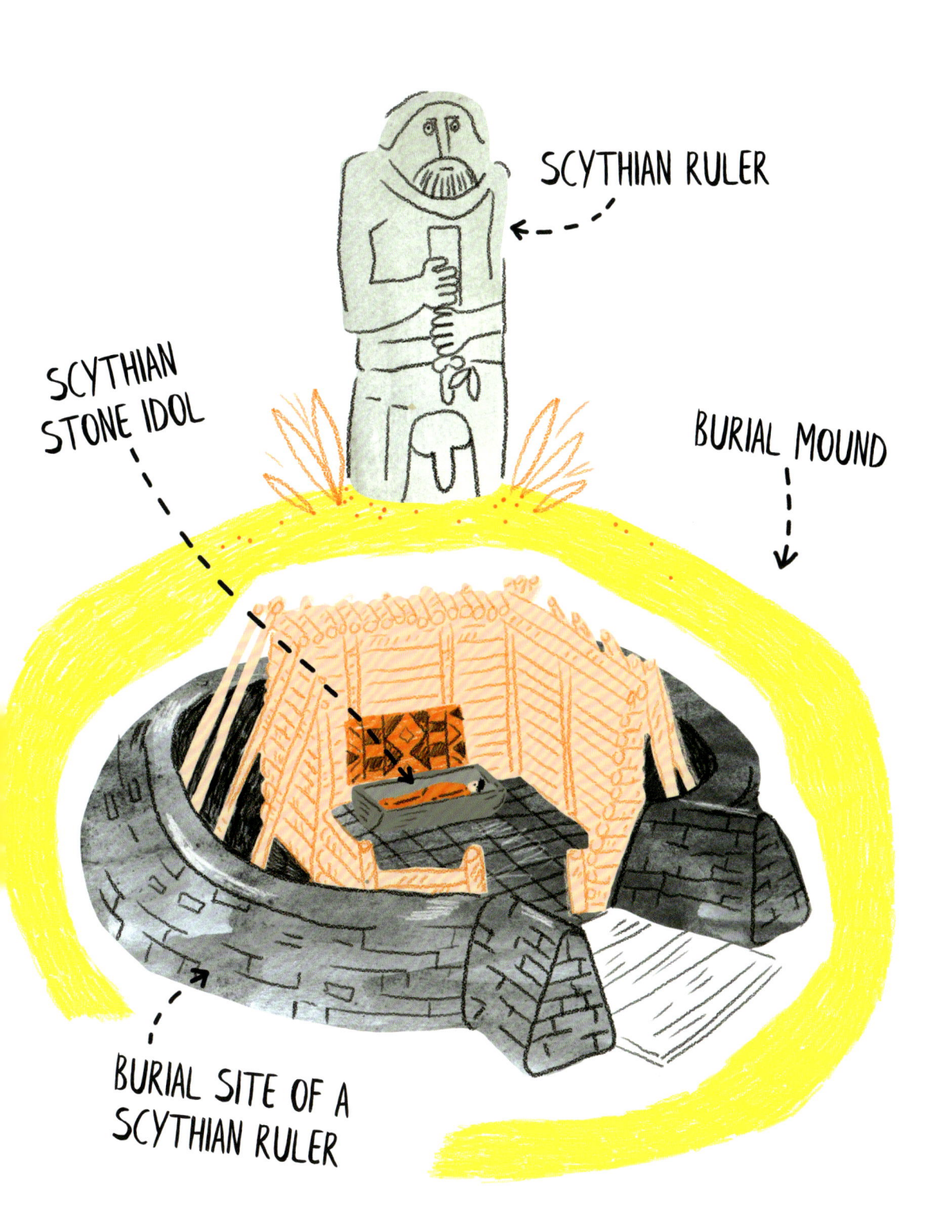

SCYTHIAN STONE IDOL

BURIAL MOUND

BURIAL SITE OF A SCYTHIAN RULER

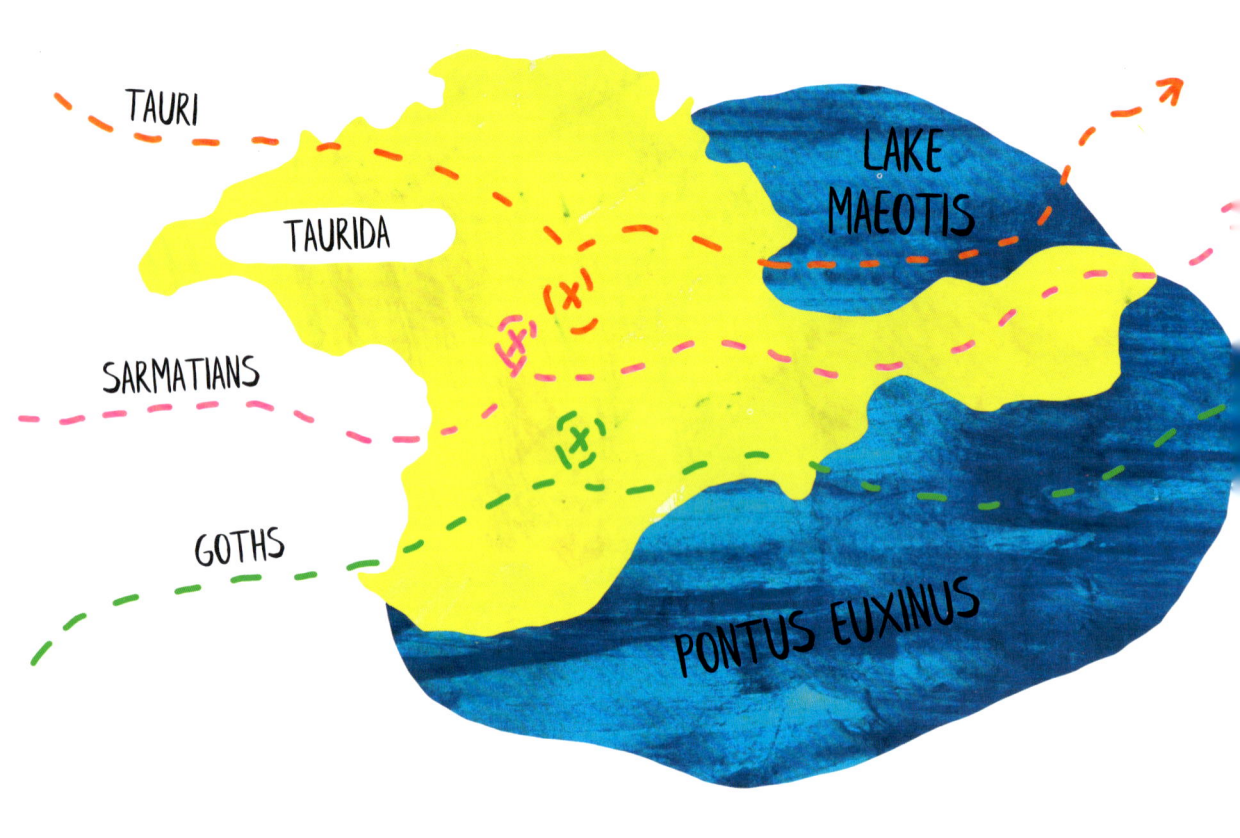

numerous city-states along the coasts of the Mediterranean and Black Seas. It's called the Ancient Greek Colonization. Once the Greeks settled down, they started trading with locals and adopted local customs. They also described the area where they lived. Greeks called the Black Sea 'Pontus Euxinus', the Azov Sea 'Lake Maeotis', and the Dnipro River 'Borysphen'. Crimea was called Taurida, since the people of Tauri lived there.

"And then, in the fourth century BCE, the Sarmatians arrived. Other Greek historians wrote about it. **The Sarmatians defeated Great Scythia, so only Lesser Scythia in the Crimea was left. The Sarmatians were nomads, just like the Scythians, and they also lived a nomadic life in tribes**. But they never established their own state. Sarmatians were skillful warriors. **Young Sarmatian**

women fought, too. The Greeks wrote that Sarmatian girls got married only after they'd killed three enemies."

"But why is it a miracle that young women were fighting?" Dmytryk said, scratching his head. "Some Scythian girls fought, too, didn't they? You just mentioned their queen."

"These are exceptions," Sashko said. "Most people in the world believed that women were not fit for war and could not fight."

"They should see my mum! What a weird thing to say!"

"And what did the Sarmatians do?" Yasia wondered, pulling an image of a Sarmatian girl up on her screen. "Did they trade with the Greeks as well?"

"Not at all. They were mostly fighting. Perhaps that's why we know much less about the Sarmatians than about the Scythians. After the Roman Empire conquered the Greek colonies in these territories, the Sarmatians were mostly looting the lands along its borders. They also blackmailed Rome for money, threatening to attack them."

"Sounds like a great business," Aliye said, laughing. "You do nothing and get paid for it!"

"This kind of business was popular," Sashko said. "**In the second century, the Goths arrived in Ukraine**. They gained the support of the local Slavs, defeated the Sarmatians and forced Rome to pay money to *them* for not attacking its borders."

"My head is spinning from all these tribes coming and going," Yasia admitted.

"It will get even worse," Aliye said.

"Could we talk about it next time, perhaps?" Yasia begged. "Let me figure things out with all these people first!"

(4)

4 A NATION AT THE CROSSROADS OF WORLDS

Coming home from school, Dmytryk saw that Viktor, his father's old friend, had come for a visit.

"But why can't you come, Serhiy?" Viktor grumbled. "It's been so long since we all got together."

"Olesia is down with a cold. How can I leave her alone?" his father said. "And then I have to go shopping at the weekend – Dmytryk needs a new jacket and trainers."

"Your wife should be doing all that," Viktor said. "It's not a man's job."

"Really?" His father laughed and turned to Dmytryk. "Would you like some buckwheat kasha with a cutlet? Or maybe soup? There's still some in the fridge. Look, Viktor, these kids are mine, just as much as they are Kateryna's. We share our responsibilities."

"'Share', you say? Okay, where's their mother, then?" his friend quipped.

"She's defending Ukraine on the frontline. So that our children will grow up in an independent and democratic country. Would you like some soup, Viktor?" Dmytryk's father said. It was hard to throw him off balance.

"It's no job for a woman." Viktor wasn't going to give up. "Women have never fought in wars. Their job is to take care of kids at home."

"It's not true! They did!" Dmytryk protested. He'd already set his

SHE'S DEFENDING UKRAINE ON THE FRONTLINE

WOMEN HAVE NEVER FOUGHT IN WARS

THEY DID!

THEN

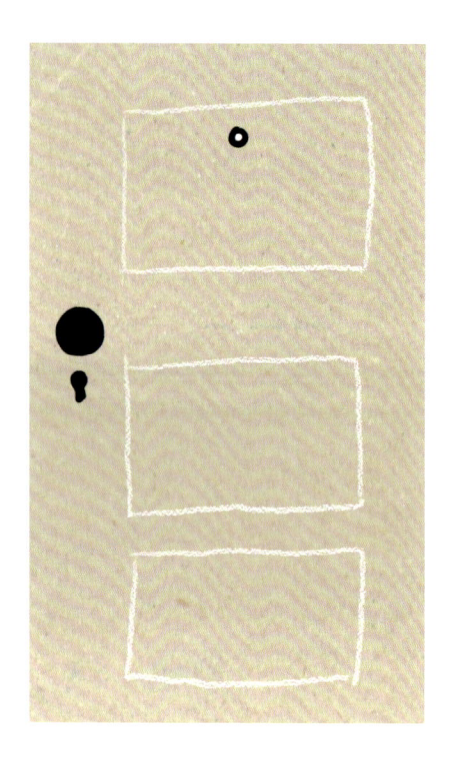

backpack down, washed his hands and got ready to eat his soup. But now he put his spoon aside and started telling him about Scythian and Sarmatian female warriors, about Princess Olga and the girls of the Polovtsi tribe. He was planning to tell his friends all about them that night.

"Stupid fairy tales," Viktor said, cutting him short. "I just don't understand why you didn't divorce her right after she joined the army. What kind of woman wants to go to war? Only a crazy one."

A dead silence fell. Dmytryk looked from his father to his father's friend. Serhiy put a ladle aside and took off his apron.

"What about men, Viktor? Are you saying that only crazy men want to fight in the war? Do you mean that everyone who's now defending their homeland is crazy?"

"No, you got me wrong."

"Then be careful what you say to me. That's an insult to me and my family."

"What did I say that was so terrible?" Viktor seethed with anger. Serhiy sighed.

"You'd better leave, Viktor. And don't come here again. Ever."

Dmytryk's father shut the door after his friend left, enraged, and sighed a heavy sigh again.

"Things happen, son. Even with old friends … What about your buddies? Do they tease you because your mother is fighting?"

"Of course not!" Dmytryk said, his

YOU ARE LUCKIER WITH FRIENDS THAN ME

eyes wide open. "They asked me to say hello to Mama and thank her."

His father smiled.

"You are luckier with friends than me."

Yasia gave her friends a long, hard stare.

"So, what happened after the Goths?"

"The Great Migration, a period where lots of different tribes moved around our region," Aliye announced happily. "And **then the Western Roman Empire broke up**, the period called Antiquity ended and the Middle Ages began."

"Are you kidding?" Yasia groaned. "What migration? How many people moved where?"

"Lots of them. The Slavs. Your ancestors."

"Were they your ancestors, too?" Sashko wondered.

"I am a *kırımlı* (the name Crimean Tatars use to identify themselves)," Aliye said. "But let's talk about your ancestors for now.

"So, **the Great Migration happened around the second century**. Over that period, lots of peoples moved from Asia to Europe, and from Eastern Europe to Western Europe. Most of them passed through today's Ukrainian lands. The Goths were driven out by the Huns, followed by the Bulgars, the Avars and later the Khazars.

"Around this time, the Slavic tribes started to settle down across Europe.

KHORYV → **SHCHEK** → **KYI** **LYBID** ←

THE ANTES ALLIANCE

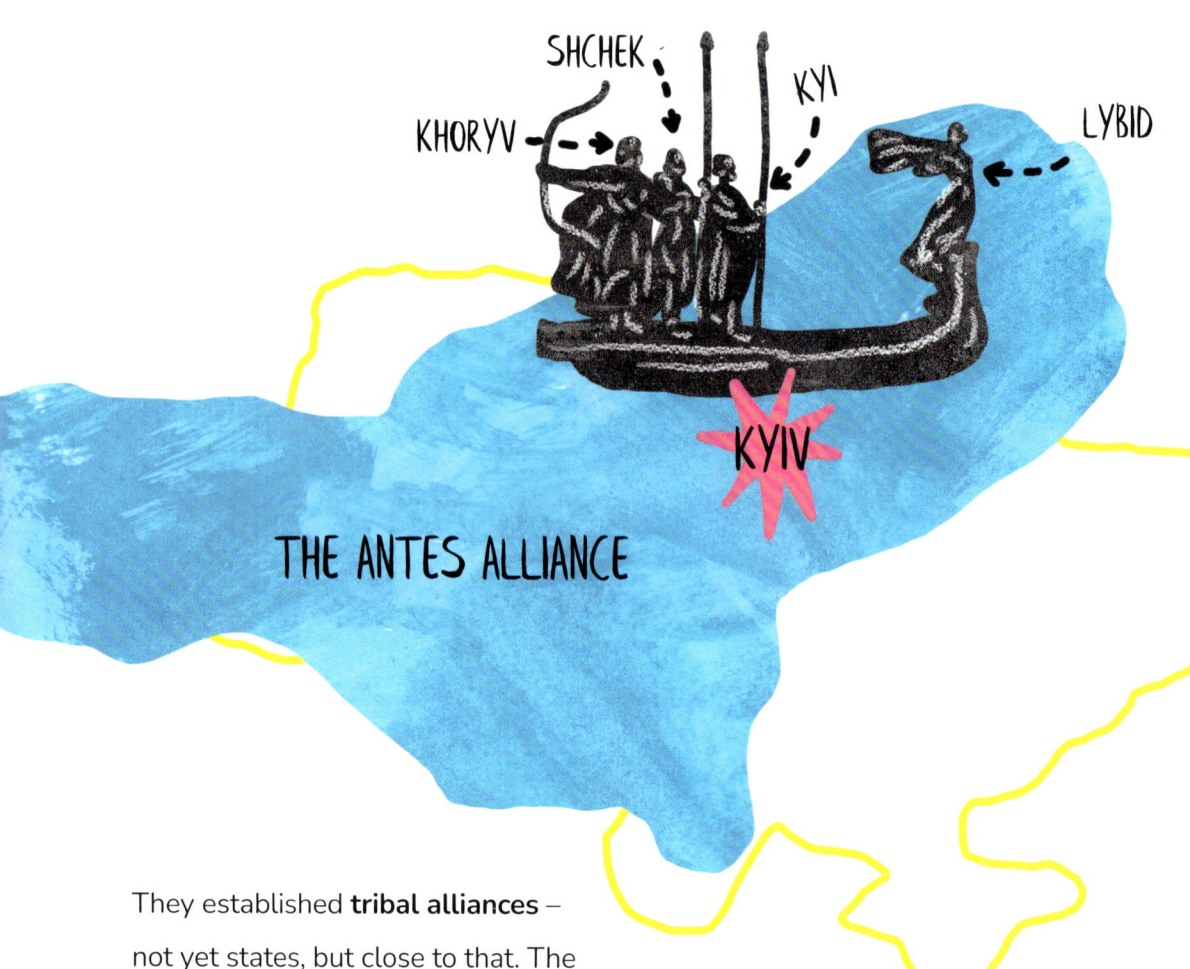

★ **KYIV**

They established **tribal alliances** – not yet states, but close to that. The Slavs were skillful warriors, but then the moment came when they had to build their own state to protect themselves and their families.

"Some Slavic tribes joined together to form the Antes Alliance in the sixth century CE. The Antes Alliance was the first of its kind on our lands but it collapsed after the long war with the Avars. It was roughly around that time, in the fifth century, that Kyiv was founded by the legendary brothers Kyi, Shchek and Khoryv and their sister Lybid.

"At this time in Europe, new trade routes were emerging – in particular, **the route from the Baltic Sea to Byzantium (Constantinople)** down the Dnipro river. This route was particularly important to the Varangians (also known as Vikings). Varangians **were warriors from what is today Sweden, Norway and Denmark**, while the Greeks fought for the Byzantine Empire – the eastern provinces of the collapsing Roman Empire, the largest and the richest country in Europe.

"**Kyiv became an important trade center** and a destination for merchants and travelers. They traveled not only down the Dnipro but also from the east and the west, along the Volga trade route. Some of the Varangian military leaders decided to conquer Kyiv. "

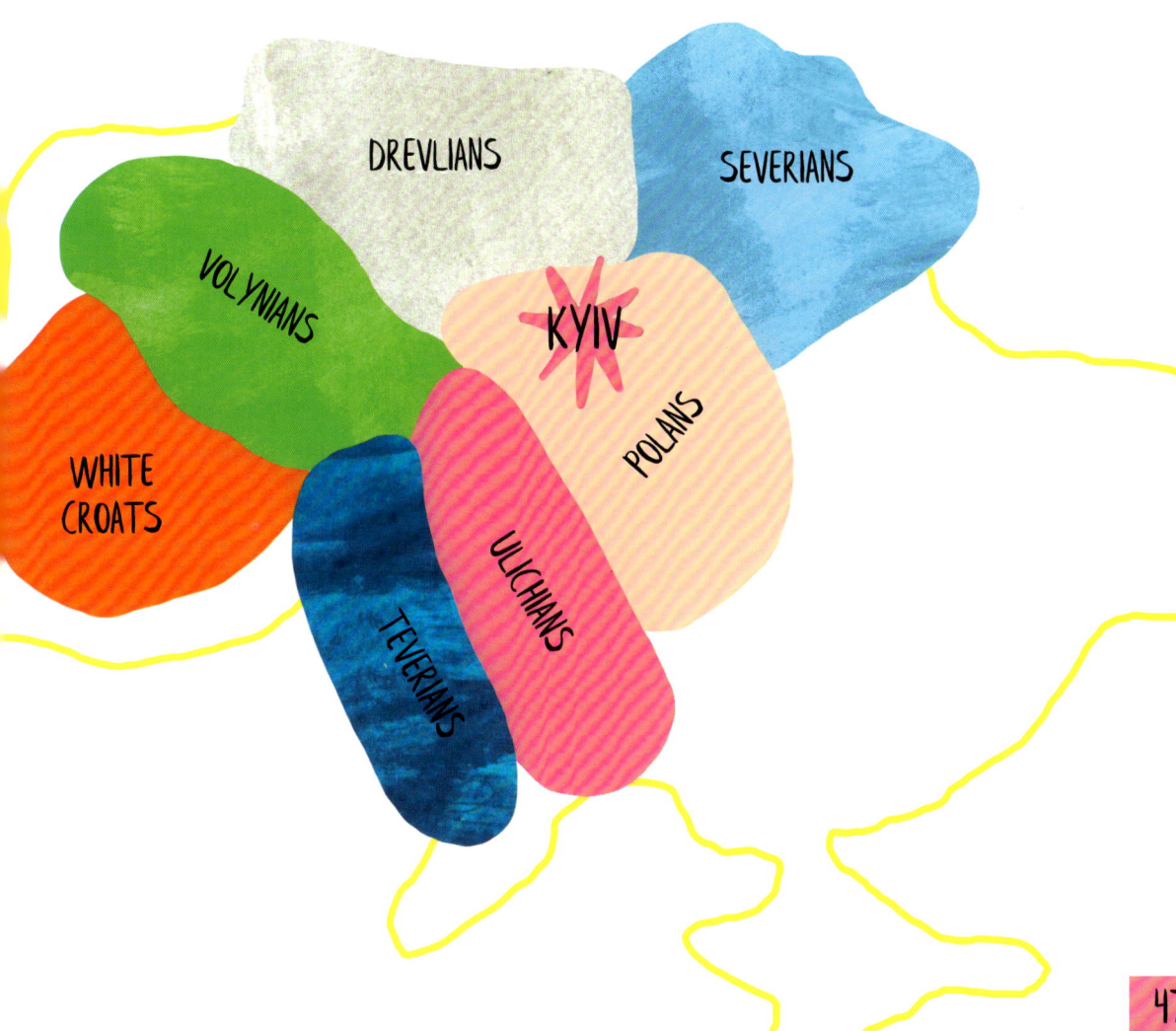

DREVLIANS

SEVERIANS

VOLYNIANS

KYIV

POLANS

WHITE CROATS

ULICHIANS

TEVERIANS

"Why?" Dmytryk asked, frowning. Sashko scratched his nose.

"Rich towns paid lots of taxes to their rulers. Not in cash, though. Mostly in expensive furs, beeswax, honey and grain. The merchants who shipped amber from the Baltic Sea coast or silver from the Khazar Khaganate paid their dues, too. The princes loaded those 'taxes' onto their ships and headed to the Byzantine Empire. If you conquered two large trade towns, let's say Novgorod in the north and Kyiv in the south, you'd collect twice as much taxes. This area expanded and later became known as Kyivan Rus – a state along the route from the Varangians to the Greeks.

"But the local tribes were not going to accept that quietly. They rebelled and wanted the state to be of some use to them, not just to collect taxes. And the state began to change. At first, the Varangians became less like the Varangians and more like the Slavs…"

"How so?"

"This is how," Aliye said. She'd dropped her pen and crawled under the table to look for it. "Princess Helga and Prince Ingvar named their son Svyatoslav. They adopted local customs and language. Then the state grew into something bigger than collecting dues once a year. The princes started to mint (make) coins, build roads and care about justice. And when Volodymyr, Svyatoslav's son, took the throne, Kyivan Rus became a real state."

"Volodymyr? **The one who converted Kyivan Rus in 988 and adopted Christianity as the main religion**?"

"Yeah. I should say, though, that many Christians had been there even before the mass baptism. And quite a few people remained pagans after that. **It's just that from then on, chronicles were written by Christian monks.**"

VARANGIANS

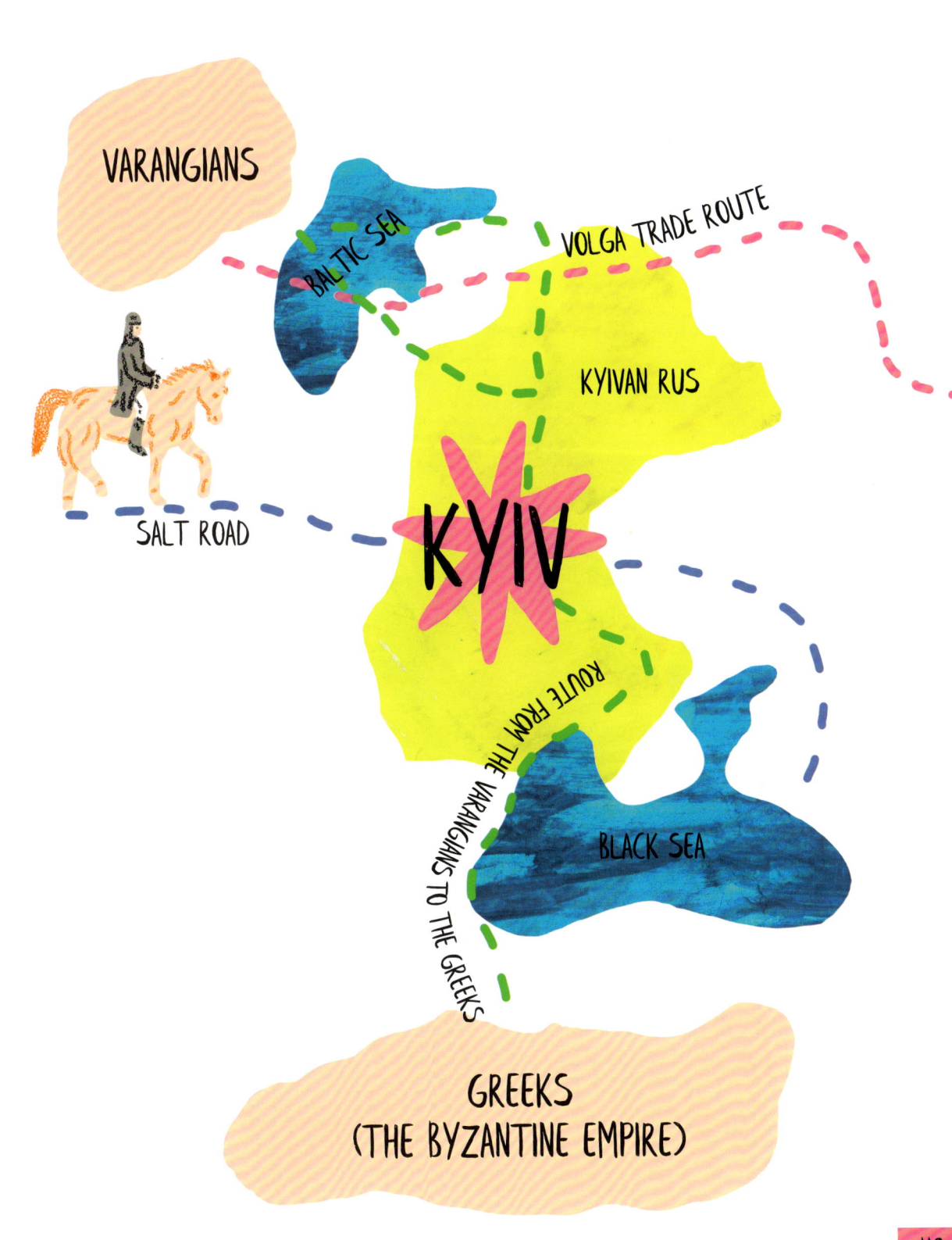

BALTIC SEA

VOLGA TRADE ROUTE

KYIVAN RUS

SALT ROAD

KYIV

ROUTE FROM THE VARANGIANS TO THE GREEKS

BLACK SEA

GREEKS
(THE BYZANTINE EMPIRE)

49

CHERNIHIV

ST ELLIAS CHURCH

ST BORYS AND GLIB CATHEDRAL

"**He also married Anna, a Byzantine princess**," Yasia said, her face lighting up. "It was so cool, because her grandpa, Constantine VII Porphyrogenitus, compiled a treatise about ruling the empire where he stressed that Byzantium rulers had never married their princesses off to the rulers of neighbouring states and would never do so. They considered all their neighbours savages and barbarians. That's why."

"And Volodymyr's son, **Yaroslav, compiled a legal code**, *Rus Justice*, which served as the basis for Kyiv's laws. And his daughters became queens of different European states. Some buildings built in his time survive to this day, including Kyiv's St Sophia Cathedral."

"Right! We have many of them

in Chernihiv. For example, **St Elias Church** or **St Borys and Glib Cathedral**," Yasia said. She quickly clicked on the mouse and pulled up the photos. "I can show you around when you come for a visit."

Sashko smiled and looked down at his phone screen.

"And then there's St Sophia Cathedral in Kyiv, Church of the Savior at Berestove and many others. I wrote down their names. But these are all large public buildings. I wish the houses where people lived had survived, too. All we have now are reconstructions in the museums."

"I'd love to go there," Dmytryk said dreamily. Sashko shrugged.

"No problem. We'll go to those museums and to Chernihiv and Kyiv, too. And to many other places."

KYIV

ST MICHAEL CATHEDRAL

CHURCH OF THE SAVIOR AT BERESTOVE

KYIV-PECHERSK LAVRA

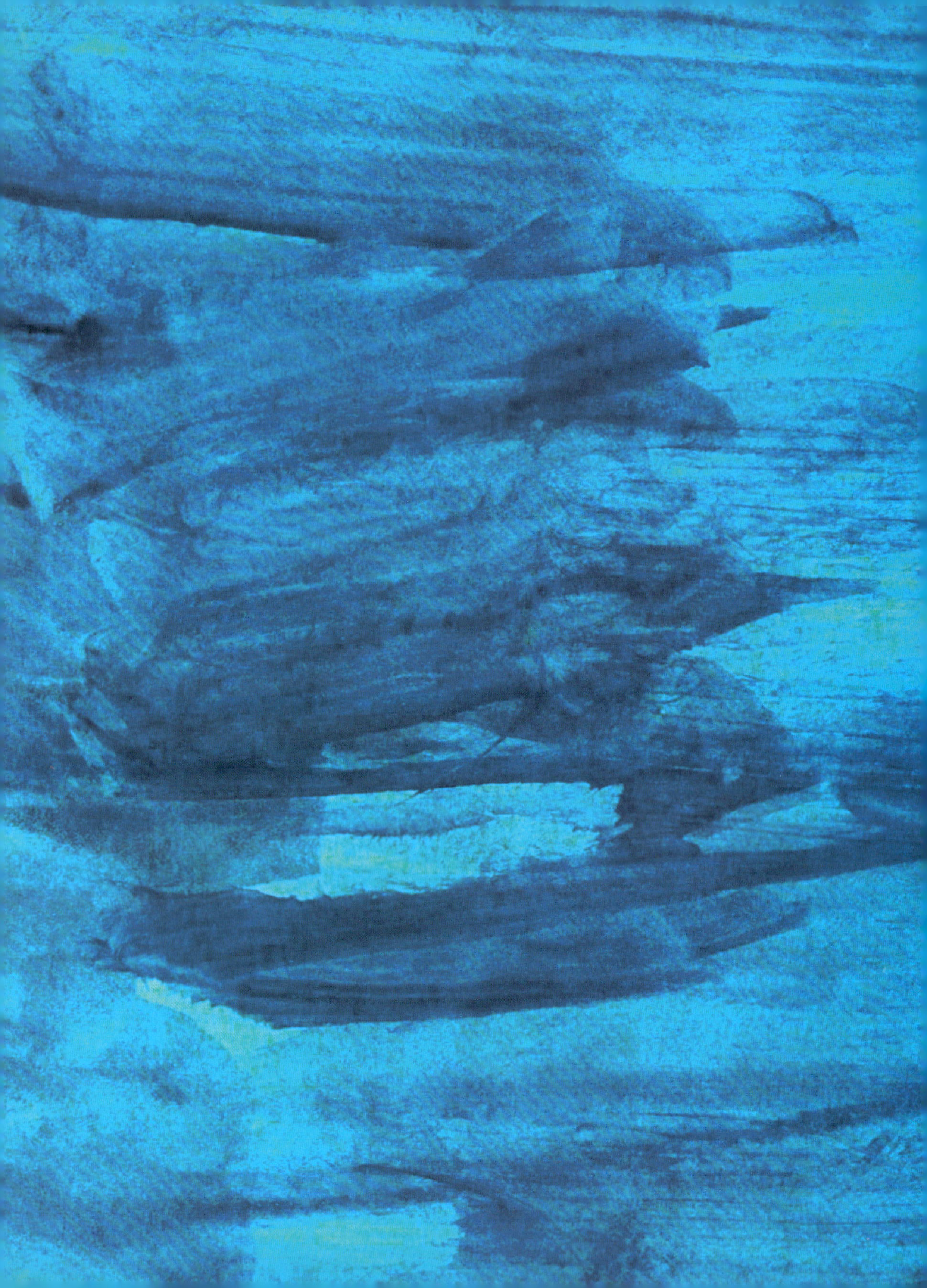

5

5. THE KINGDOM OF RUS

Yasia's parents often went on business trips – usually in turns but sometimes both at the same time. In which case, they took Yasia and her older sister, Oksana, to their grandpa, or grandpa came to them. But when one of their daughters had her birthday, their parents always stayed at home. Always.

So, when Yasia overheard her mother and father discussing another business trip scheduled sometime soon, she felt the ground slipping from under her feet. Of course, she knew that there were all kinds of situations. Something might come up, and her parents may have to leave them, even on a holiday. But they should warn them at least!

For a few days, Yasia was sad and withdrawn. She quarreled with her sister: she just couldn't bring herself to tell Oksana about their parents' decision. She also snapped at her mother and father.

"What's happened, Yasia?" mother asked at last. "I see that you're upset. Is there anything you'd like to tell me?"

Finally, Yasia exploded.

"Perhaps there's something *you* would like to tell me?" she burst out. "For example, about your plans to go away for my birthday and say nothing to me about it?!"

She rushed into her room and was just about to slam the door when her mother laughed:

FATHER   MOTHER

55

SUMY REGION

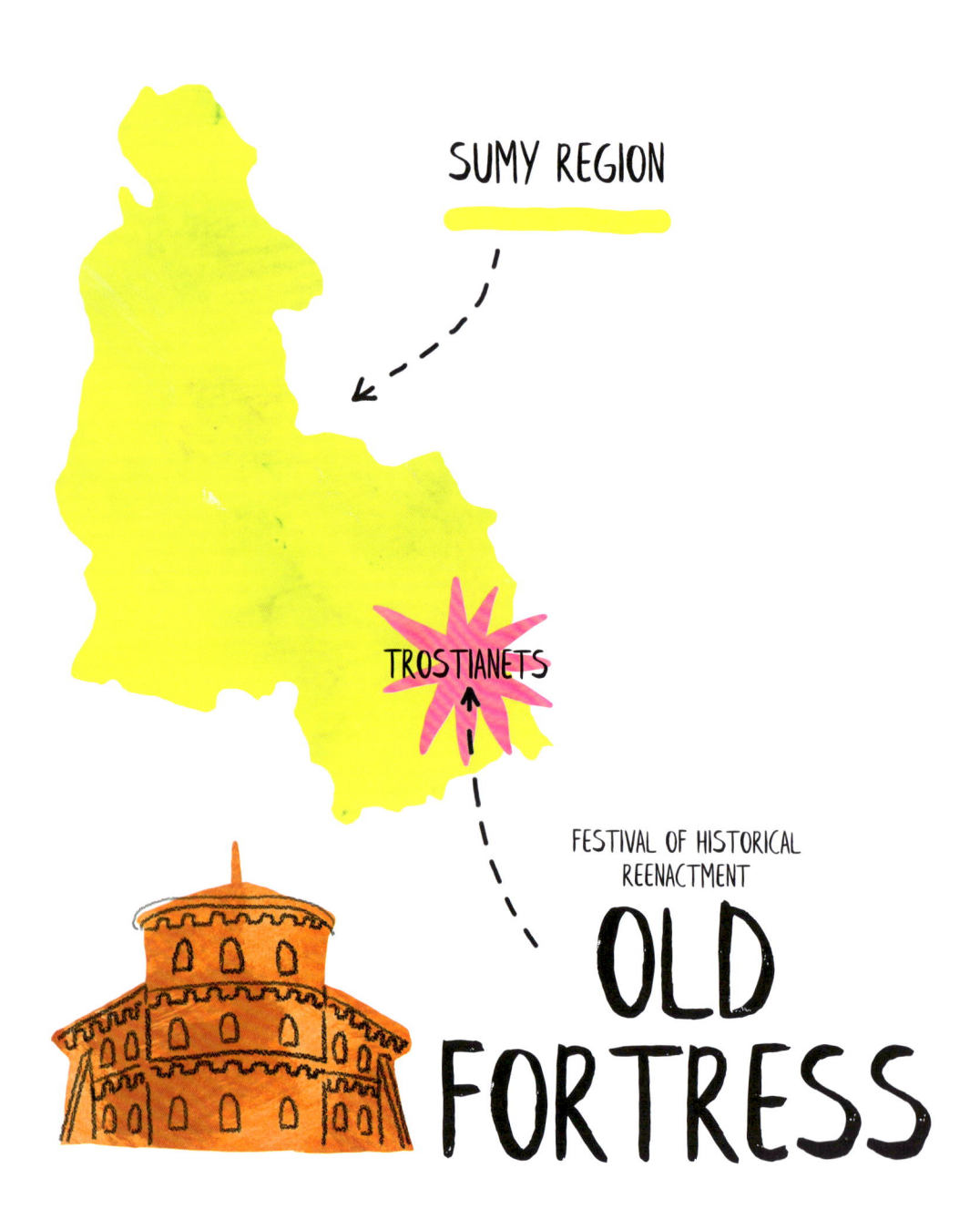

TROSTIANETS

FESTIVAL OF HISTORICAL REENACTMENT

OLD FORTRESS

"You've got it wrong, sweetheart!" she said. "We just wanted to surprise you!"

The door stopped a moment before slamming, and Yasia turned around warily:

"What kind of surprise?"

"Well ... you won't tell Dad that I gave our secret away, will you? So, we saw that you've become interested in history and decided to take you and Oksana to the festival of historical reenactment that starts soon."

Yasia blinked, confused, and wrinkled her forehead again.

"Now I feel like a fool," she said.

Mother came up to her and hugged her.

"Me too, honey. But I hope it won't spoil our trip."

"Has anyone figured out what '**feudalism**' is all about?" Sashko wondered. He did not expect anyone to know – it was written all over his face.

"A bit," Yasia said hesitantly. "I asked the reenactors about it. The thing is that in medieval Europe, the power of kings or princes depended on the personal pledges of their lords – people who owned land. Loyal service to the king, such as supporting him in a war. Lords were defended by paid knights, while peasants worked the land and had to give a percentage of their crops to the lords. Serfs were not free and had to work the land in return for food and shelter.

"Feudalism flourished during times of conflict, when nations were still being created from the fragments of ancient empires. Although it varied in different countries, feudalism was replaced by more centralised government, usually a powerful monarch, aided by an elite group of nobles and advisers.

"In Kyivan Rus, feudal fragmentation started with the trade

route from the Varangians to the Greeks falling out of use. But in the twelfth and thirteenth centuries, the same things were happening all over Europe. Countries broke down into pieces and united back again. Kyivan Rus began to unite, too – this time through connections between autonomous principalities, not around the trade route."

"But it was no longer Kyivan Rus," Sashko said, after looking it up online. "A new state had appeared by that time – **the Principality of Galicia–Volhynia**. Here, look at the states listed on the Ukrainian history portal."

Yasia nodded her head.

"That principality emerged after other Rus principalities united. It was ruled by a dynasty whose principals were direct descendants of Volodymyr the Great. They even called themselves **the Kingdom of Rus** in their documents."

Sashko frowned, and Dmytryk quickly asked:

"So, they were a kingdom?"

"That's right," Sashko said. "Ever since the Pope refused to help Danylo Halytskyi in his fight against **the Mongol Empire** but sent him a crown instead."

"It didn't matter anyway as the Mongols from Central Asia invaded," Aliye said, making a sour face. "They conquered Kyiv in late 1240."

"Yes," Yasia said, opening a map of the Mongol Empire. "They conquered lots of countries, including, after Rus, Poland and Hungary. They didn't stay there for long, though."

"We learned about it in school," Sashko said, rubbing his forehead. "Rus was **fragmented** into **autonomous principalities**, and they did not want to help each other. That's why they lost."

"They didn't want to help each other? Really? But **in 1223, they all got together on the Kalka River to**

THE GRAND
PRINCE OF KYIV

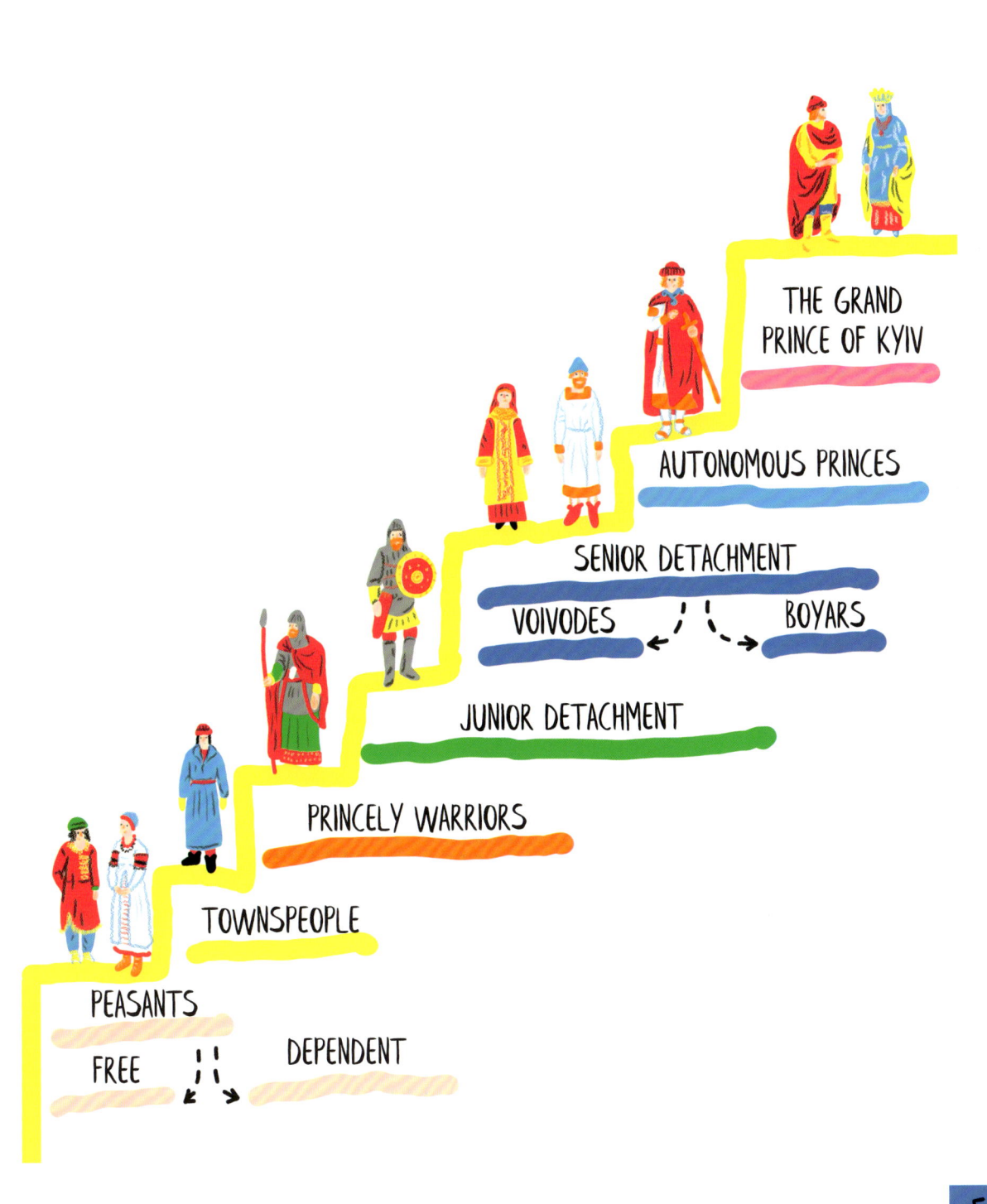

AUTONOMOUS PRINCES

SENIOR DETACHMENT

VOIVODES ⇿ BOYARS

JUNIOR DETACHMENT

PRINCELY WARRIORS

TOWNSPEOPLE

PEASANTS

FREE ⇿ DEPENDENT

THE PRINCIPALITY OF GALICIA–VOLHYNIA

VOLODYMYR

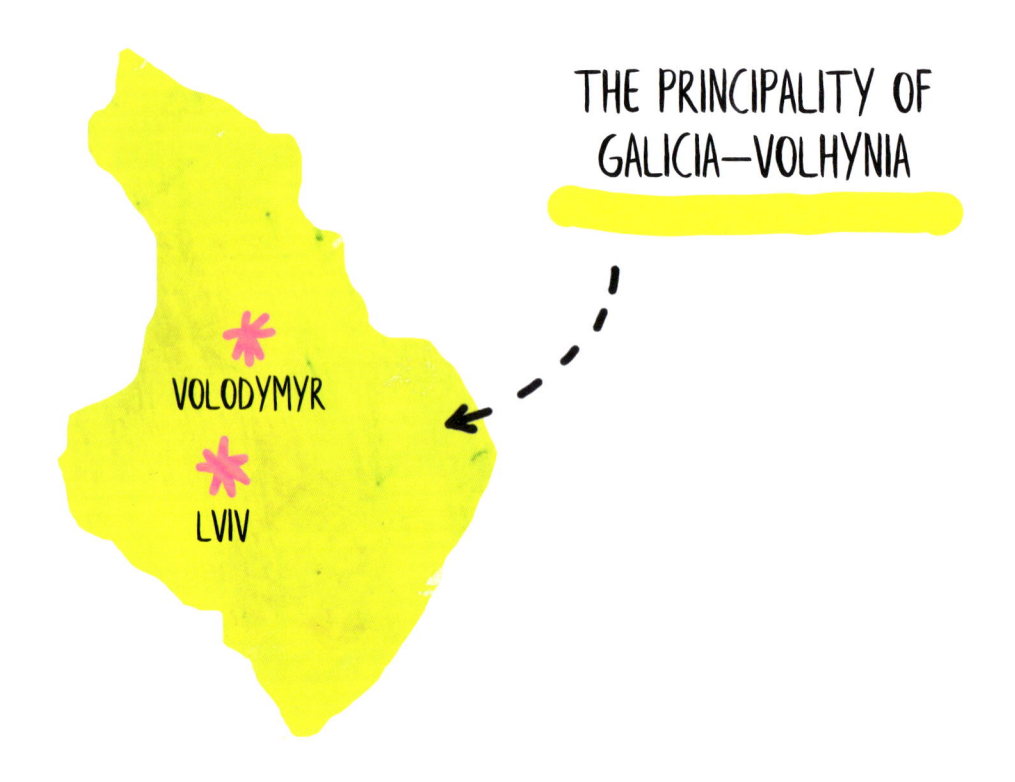

LVIV

help their neighbours, nomadic Polovtsians, in the battle with the Mongols," Yasia remarked.

"And they lost."

"Just like all the other countries that the Mongols conquered. And there was no feudal fragmentation in those lands – for example, in Khorezm."

"Why did they lose, then?"

Yasia pulled a face.

"It seems that people in Europe and the Middle

THE UKRAINIAN ARMY

RUSYCHI + POLOVTSIANS

East just didn't know how to fight with them. The Mongols were strong and fast and, after conquering China, they got lots of weapons and mastered new tactics and strategies. People didn't have enough time to invent a good strategy to defeat them – even the rulers of Rus who'd been enemies or friends with the Polovtsians, militant nomads, for two centuries."

"Anyways," Aliye spoke up. "After their defeat on the Kalka River, the Rus principalities lived in peace for some time. The Mongols didn't go any further – they had to return home. Danylo Halytskyi had just regained control over the Principality of Galicia–Volhynia, which had rebelled after the death

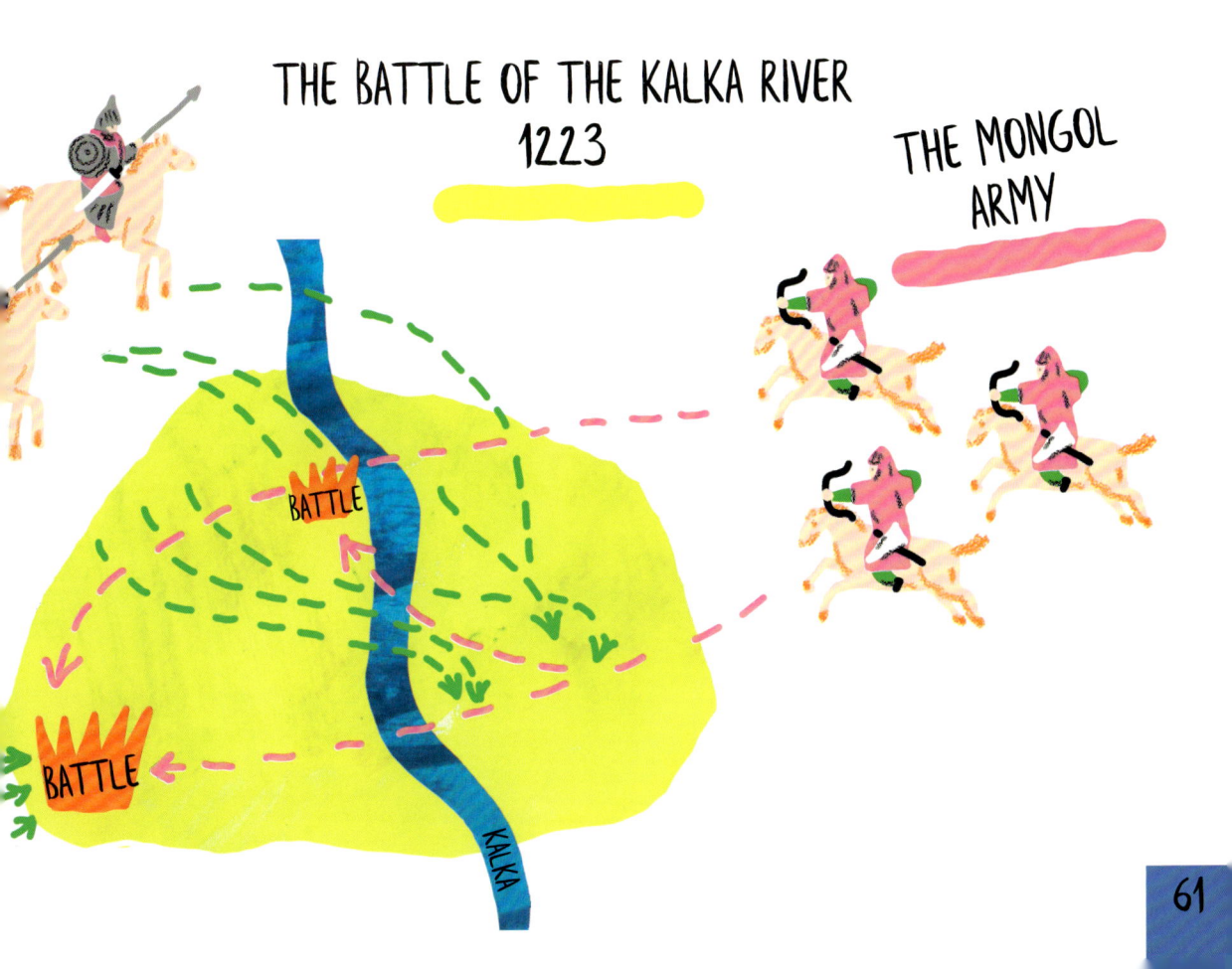

THE BATTLE OF THE KALKA RIVER 1223

THE MONGOL ARMY

BATTLE

BATTLE

KALKA

of his father, Roman Mstyslavych. He'd pushed its borders up to Kyiv when he was warned that the Mongol army was marching toward Rus again. It was in late 1237. **And in early 1241, the Mongols entered the Polish lands**.

After the Mongol invasion, Danylo had to swear allegiance to the khan (Mongol ruler) but he looked to his western neighbours for support. He had his sons marry into the ruling families of Hungary, Austria and Lithuania and he even accepted a crown from Pope Innocent in return for recognizing him as head of the church. Although little help was forthcoming, Danylo managed to drive the Mongols out of Volhynia in about 1257. However, they returned in 1260 but ruled mostly indirectly and collected money as taxes.

THE PRINCIPALITY OF CHERNIHIV

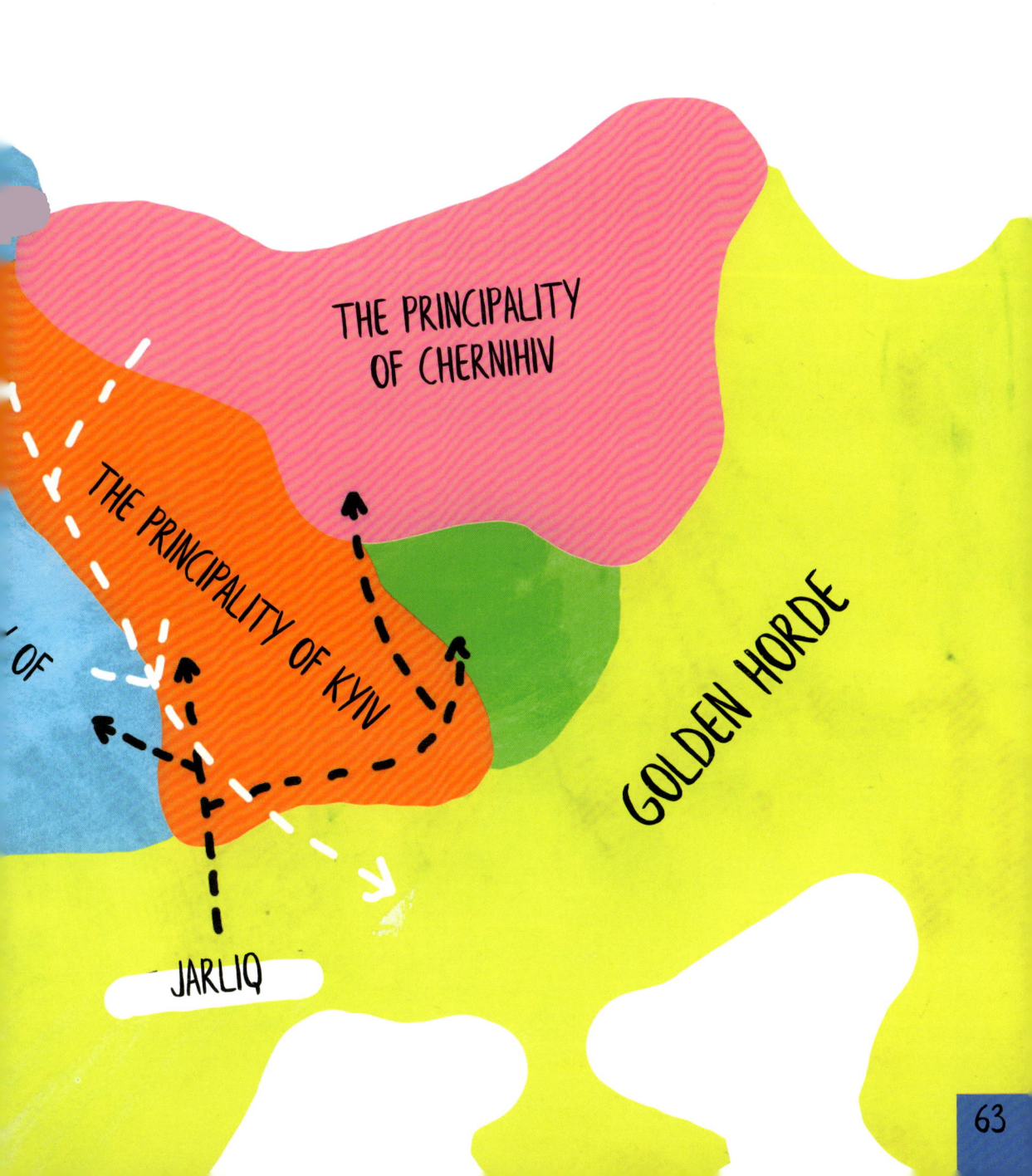

THE PRINCIPALITY OF KYIV

GOLDEN HORDE

JARLIQ

6

6 THE AGE OF BIG CHANGES

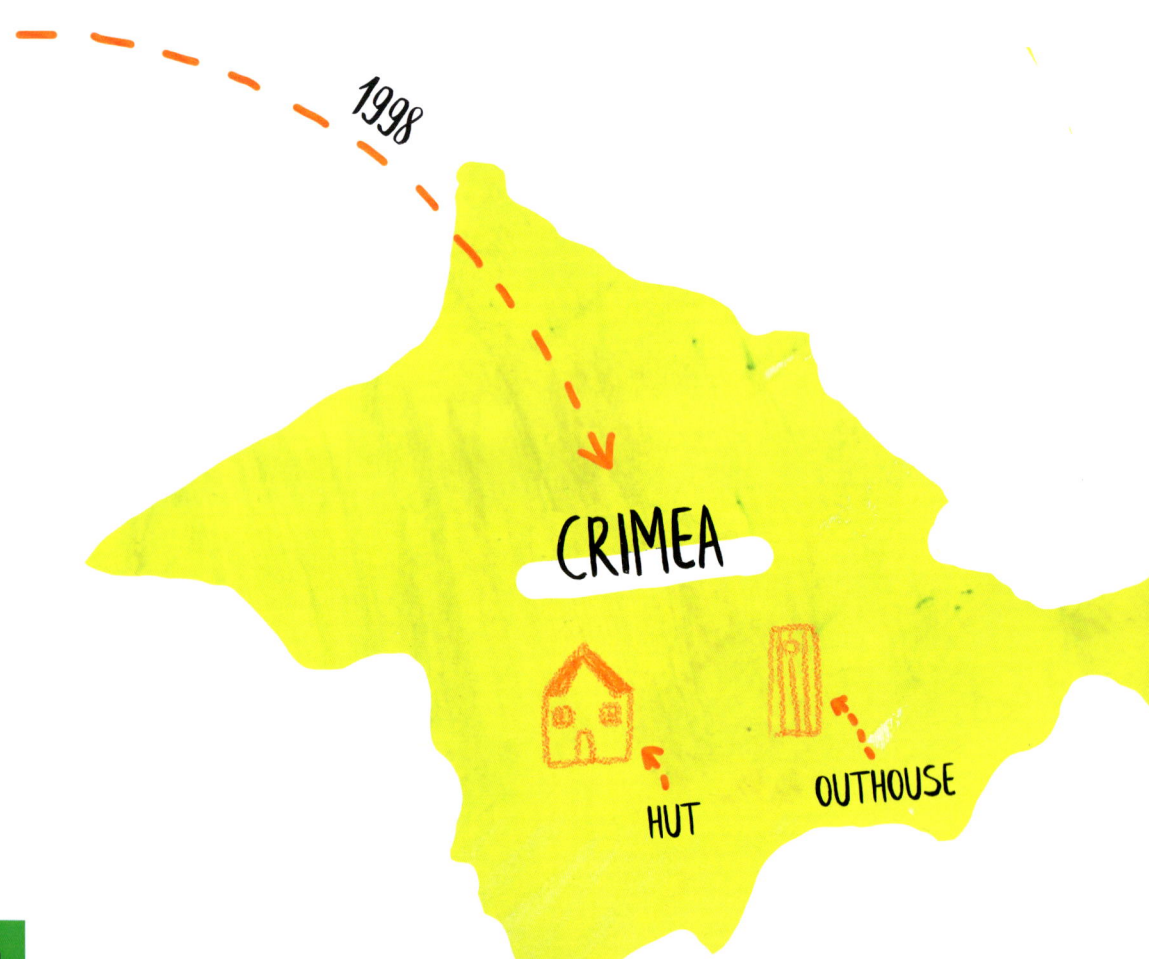

1998

CRIMEA

HUT

OUTHOUSE

"I already told you, *kızım*, that I can tell you about the birds that lived on the shores of the Parathetys. But if you need to know when the Crimean Khanate was founded, you'd better ask your mother."

"Does Mama really know about it?" Aliye asked, surprised.

"Niyara!" Rustem called. "Our daughter doesn't believe that you're good not only at software engineering but at history too!"

"I didn't say that," Aliye said, giving him a stare. Her mother came into the kitchen and went over to the pan with the *sarburma* (meat pie) that her father had just taken out of the oven.

"You know, honey, I don't think I would be a software engineer if not for history," Niyara said with a wink.

"How so?"

"It just happened that way." Niyara put a piece of pie on her plate and ushered her daughter to the living room. "As you know, I was born in exile. My family was able to return to Crimea only after Ukraine gained independence. I was nine at the time, and it was an ordeal for me…" Niyara paused, turning over a piece of half-eaten *sarburma* in her hand. "The thing is that we did not feel welcome in Crimea. The houses seized from Crimean Tatars had been given over to other people. Our mountains and villages were renamed. They hated us for daring

I DON'T THINK I WOULD BE A SOFTWARE ENGINEER IF NOT FOR HISTORY

HACI GIRAY

to return to our homeland. Our family lived in a cramped makeshift hut with an outhouse. And it was a great arrangement, really, since **many families lived in tents**."

Niyara took another bite and, chewing and swallowing it, continued her story:

"I was a quiet, homely girl. In school in Uzbekistan, I never got into fights with my classmates, and I got good grades. But here, teachers gave me low grades on purpose and looked at me with disgust. My classmates called me names, yelled at me, telling me to go back where I came from, and ripped up my notebooks. They even cut up my backpack. When I came home that day, I couldn't help myself and started yelling at my grandma. I shouted that we shouldn't have returned to Crimea. That we no longer belonged there. That her stubborn desire to return to her homeland only caused all kinds of trouble. I could see that my grandma felt upset by my shouting.

"But she didn't react. Instead, she said: 'Hacı Giray, founder of the Crimean Khanate, was born in exile, and his enemies forced him to leave Crimea many times. His allies betrayed him, but he would not give up. He was captured, but each time he waited for the right moment to escape. We cannot give up until we try as hard as he did.'

"After that incident, I developed a strong interest in the history of our people. Its knowledge gave me the strength to resist bullying in school. And when I grew up, I enrolled in the university, in the program I wanted – even though fifteen years ago, it was believed that mathematics was not a suitable subject for girls to study."

"Argh, so many different countries and peoples fighting each other again," Yasia grumbled. "But you know what? I think I've figured it all out."

"Seriously?" Dmytryk said, laughing. "Can you remember all the participants of the civil war in the Golden Horde then? I got mixed up right away."

"Well, not all of them," Yasia said and wrinkled her nose. "General Mamay seems to be the only one I remember."

Sashko looked at Aliye, who was unusually quiet, and said:

"Could we just briefly talk about the things happening in the fourteenth century?"

Dmytryk nodded.

"**Sure. In 1340, Galician boyars (nobles) poisoned Yuri II Boleslav, the last prince of the Principality of Galicia–Volhynia.**"

Sashko whistled.

"What did they have against him?"

"We can't be sure. Maybe they wanted someone else to be the ruler."

"**By the mid-fourteenth century,**

the Ukranian territories were ruled by three different foreign powers: the Mongols (also known as the Golden Horde and Tatars in Europe), Lithuania and Poland."

"The Great Duchy of Lithuania was a really fascinating case," Dmytryk said, interrupting him. "It entered the historical scene as a small, insignificant country but immediately grew into a large and powerful player. It all started with the Great Jam, **a civil war in the Golden Horde that lasted for half a century**. Oh, wait. No, it began with the Lithuanian prince Gediminas marrying the Polotsk princess Jaune. He annexed the Polotsk principality – present-day Belarusian lands.

But the story was far from over: the children of Jaune and Gediminas were the blood descendants of the early Rus princes and could even lay claims to the Kyiv throne. Their son Algirdas did just that, becoming the grand duke. Right at that time, the Great Jam broke out in the Golden Horde."

"Right!" Yasia exclaimed. "Khan Berdibek was killed, and his son-in-law, Mamay, a Polovtsian and son of the ruler of the town of…"

"Solkhat," Aliye said, helping her out. "We call it Eski Qırım – **Old Crimea**. It was the **capital of Crimea** back then."

"Right. So, Mamay, who was a *beklarbek* – it was a super high office, making him the country's third most powerful person – and Khan Berdibek's son-in-law, refused to obey and supported another khan (ruler). And it just carried on – for half a century."

Dmytryk nodded.

"And Algirdas decided that it was a great time to take a piece of land owned by the Golden Horde," he said. "He even struck a deal with Mamay, because Mamay's opponents were ruling the Ukrainian territories at that point. Algirdas

GEDIMINAS

JAUNĖ

ALGIRDAS

won back territory after territory, and in 1362, he defeated three Nogai Tatar princes at the Battle of the Blue Waters. The Nogays were the greatest power in those lands, so after that victory, the Grand Duchy of Lithuania conquered almost all the Ukrainian territories.

Lithuania gave Rus its ruling dynasty, and the descendants of Gediminas became autonomous princes. In its turn, Rus – Ukrainian and Belarusian lands, that is – gave Lithuania its law and written language. Many Lithuanians also converted to Christianity at this point as well. The state got a new name, the Grand Duchy of Lithuania, Rus and Samogitia. The territories of present-day Belarus were called Lithuania, present-day Ukraine used to be called Rus, and present-day Lithuania used to be known as Samogitia."

"And what about Mamay? What happened to him?" Sashko wondered. Dmytryk only shook his head. He had no clue.

"Mamay was defeated and killed by Tokhtamysh," Yasia said, coming to his rescue. "That guy was also eager to take the khan's throne. Manzur, Mamay's son, left Crimea and moved to the territories in today's Sumy and Poltava regions. He established the Hlynsk principality there. Later, that principality peacefully

THE BATTLE OF THE BLUE WATERS 1362

THE GRAND DUCHY OF LITHUANIA

PLACE OF ASSEMBLY

BATTLE

SIEGE OF KYIV

GOLDEN HORDE

joined the Grand Duchy of Lithuania."

"And what about the Golden Horde?"

"Well, Tokhtamysh suffered defeats from two of his enemies and fled to the same place – the Grand Duchy of Lithuania. His relatives and allies followed him. I think it was in Trakai in Samogitia that the first Crimean khan was born. He was Tokhtamysh's nephew."

"Not a nephew, maybe, but a relative, for sure. Hacı Giray fought on the side of Tokhtamysh, and Tokhtamysh's daughter, Janike Khanım, called him her 'favourite orphaned relative'.

"You can't tell Hacı Giray's story without Janike. Her father married her off to his opponent, Edigey, to make peace. But the peace didn't last for long, and Janike's father and older brothers died. She was lucky to save her youngest brother, Kadir Berdi, and send him away to Crimea. But when he grew older, he also went to war against Edigey – and died during battle.

"Janike was left behind as the eldest in her family. She returned

JANIKE KHANIM'S TOMB

to Crimea. At that point, Crimea was already craving independence from the Golden Horde with its endless wars. But Janike didn't support any of her nephews – she offered her loyalty to Hacı Giray, the last member of the dynasty of former Crimean rulers. When Hacı Giray set foot on his new territories, Janike Khanım gave her 'favourite relative' a fortress, Jantym-Kale. She supported all his pursuits, even when her nephews banished him a few times from Crimea, the most influential Crimean dynasties turned away from him, and the Grand Duchy of Lithuania broke the agreement with him only to strike a deal with his enemies.

"You could say that Crimea's independence was fought back by exiles: most warriors in Hacı Giray's army were the same Tatars who once asked the Gediminid dynasty for asylum. But there were also people waiting for those exiles back in Crimea. They helped them and made sure they could always rely on them. Like Janike Khanım.

"By the way, the Crimean Khanate occupied not just part of Crimea, but also the steppes in the Black Sea region. I say 'part', because the first khan had to fight for the southern coast of Crimea with Genova, an Italian city-state that owned the coastal fortresses."

"What a story! Is there a portrait of Janike Khanım?" Sashko asked.

"No," Aliye said, shaking her head. "There's her tomb in Crimea, though."

"It would be great to go there and see it..." Dmytryk said dreamily but broke off, embarrassed, as Aliye bit her lip.

"Yes," Aliye nodded. "I wish I could go there, too ... at least once."

7

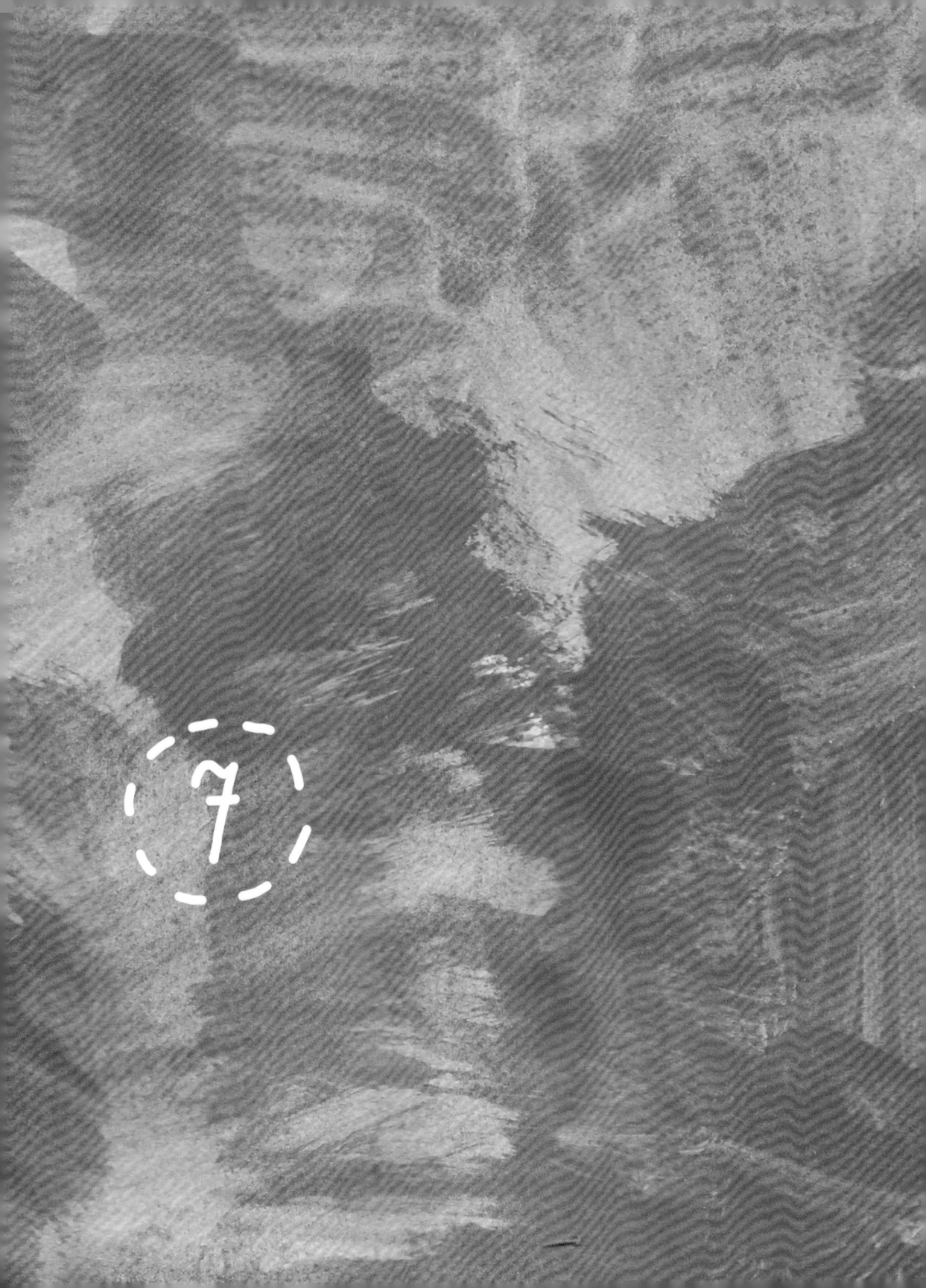

7 FROM BORDERLANDS TO THE HETMANATE

"Aliye isn't here? And she hasn't texted anything?" Sashko asked, checking the chat for the fifth time.

"As you can see!" Yasia snapped. "I have no idea what happened. Everything was okay two days ago when we talked about meeting."

Dmytryk sighed dramatically.

"A fight is all we need. Then we'll all say goodbye and leave. I have Aliye's number. Let me call her."

In a few minutes, he assured his friends that Aliye would join them soon.

"She doesn't feel like talking to anyone, but her mother persuaded her to talk to us."

"What happened?"

"Her classmates are bullying her or something."

"And what do we have to do with it?" Sashko grunted. "We're not bullies."

Dmytryk pulled a face.

"They're bullying her because she's a Crimean Tatar, and now she doesn't want to talk to any Ukrainians."

A notification flashed in the chat, and the image of a gloomy, red-eyed Aliye came up on their screens.

"What happened, Aliye?" Yasia asked her softly. "Has anyone hurt you?"

"Oh, come on! Don't pretend as if you don't know anything! You, too, are going to blame me for things that happened centuries ago, aren't you?"

"Why should we blame you?" Sashko asked, surprised. "We are friends, aren't we?"

"I also had 'friends' in my class," Aliye snapped, "until one of them decided to help me with a quest and read about the **Tatar Horde** and *yasyr*! Now the whole class won't speak to me!"

"Are they idiots?" Sashko asked.

"What? Don't you agree with them?" Aliye said. Her voice was calm, but at the end of the sentence, she sniffed.

"Of course not!" Sashko protested. "It all happened so long ago. How can anyone blame you for that?"

Dmytryk stepped in.

"It was a complicated story. I think Aliye could tell us a lot about what the Cossacks did in Crimea."

Aliye was giving them a hard stare, as if she expected them to attack her with reproaches and scorn.

"I think we're starting the wrong way," Yasia said. "First of all, we have to figure out what our ancestors thought about each

79

other. I mean, discuss the issue that brought us all here today.

"Let me start. So, **in 1569, the Grand Duchy of Lithuania united with Poland and formed the Polish–Lithuanian Commonwealth**. And in 1475, the Crimean Khanate became subordinate to the Ottoman Empire.

"They united because they wanted to, indeed, but problems popped up right away. The Poles wanted to become as close as possible, while the Lithuanian and Rus princes wanted to keep their own customs and self-government. But the threat of war with a dangerous enemy – the Tsardom of Muscovy – was looming, and they needed to search for an ally, so they signed the union treaty after all.

"On top of that, this unification opened up the possibilities of self-government to the Rus and Lithuanian nobility: three Ukrainian

THE POLISH–LITHUANIAN COMMONWEALTH

THE GRAND DUCHY OF LITHUANIA

THE KINGDOM OF POLAND

THE WILD FIELDS

THE OTTOMAN EMPIRE

THE CRIMEAN KHANATE

provinces, or voivodeships, became subjects of Poland, not Lithuania. They freed themselves from the power of autonomous princes and secured rights and privileges: the Old Ukrainian language as the state language in their territories; the inviolability of borders of the three voivodeships; and equal rights for the Orthodox Christians and Catholics, which was very important in then Catholic Poland and Europe, where the religious wars were already underway.

"Meanwhile, the Ukrainian voivodeships and the Crimean Khanate were separated by the Wild Fields, **a large expanse of steppe where no one was living**. Crimean Tatars actually passed through the Wild Fields during their military campaigns and captured prisoners – *yasyr*. They sold them later at slave markets across the Ottoman Empire. Somehow, there was never enough money in the state treasury to protect that particular border. The slave trade was still considered a decent business back then – as long as fellow countryfolk were not traded.

"Nomads travelled to the Wild Fields, too – those were free lands, not someone's private property, so they could hunt and fish there and sell their catch back home. It attracted people who wanted to improve their lives: peasants who wanted to escape from their dependency on their landlords; nobility that had lost their land; townspeople; and all kinds of adventurers.

"The nomads started to form self-defense units to protect themselves and frontier towns and villages from Tatars. The members of those units became known as Cossacks. The Polish–Lithuanian Commonwealth recruited some of them for service – those were registered Cossacks. The rest just stayed as they were.

DMYTRO VYSHNEVETSKYI

Prince Dmytro Vyshnevetskyi **built a fortress on Khortytsia island to pool them together**. It didn't stand long but became **the prototype for Zaporizhzhia Sich, the main Cossack stronghold**. Built in the lower reaches of the Dnipro River, Sich was the central Cossack fortress where they elected their chieftains and hetmans. You could say that it was the headquarters of the Cossack grassroots troops. The Cossacks even started to organize their own military campaigns against the Crimean Khanate and the Ottoman Empire."

"And it was then," Dmytryk jumped in, "that they did things that Aliye can blame our ancestors for."

"I can," Aliye said drily, "but I won't. Because I... I... I'm not such a fool as they are."

"It's just that you know history, and they never thought about the past," Dmytryk said in a soft voice.

"Aliye is not the only one who can do that," Sashko said with a sigh.

Yasia shrugged.

"Everyone can blame everyone else," she said. "We could blame Poles, for one. As soon as the dynasties of Ukrainian princes lost their power, Poles forgot that **the Orthodox and the Catholics were**

equal, as promised by the Union of Lublin. It all started peacefully: the Orthodox church declined; its priests were poorly educated and often traded church offices. To solve this problem, they tried to unite the two churches but ended up creating a third one. Now we call it the Greek Catholic Church, but back then it was called the Uniate Church. It wasn't anything bad by itself, of course – especially given that lots of new Christian movements were emerging in Europe – but the Orthodox nobility viewed it as an attempt to destroy their freedom of religion. They stood their ground. But the Poles didn't step back, either, and **limited the rights of the Orthodox townspeople** living in the territories where they had more power.

"The townspeople stood firm, too – they set up brotherhoods, opened schools and took care of the Orthodox churches. But the

ZAPORIZHZHIA SICH

most obstinate people were the Cossacks, who'd slowly grown into a powerful force. However, the Polish–Lithuanian Commonwealth didn't want to recognize it.

"The thing was that the nobility enjoyed plenty of privileges and did not pay taxes. At the same time, they could hold important government posts and own lands and dependent peasants. The gentry paid their dues for it – they were obliged to defend the borders of the Polish–Lithuanian Commonwealth. So, here come the Cossacks, who performed the duties of the gentry but didn't get the privileges they enjoyed."

"I don't think the Cossacks appreciated that," Sashko said.

"No, not really. They organized seven uprisings," Yasia said.

"Seven? Wow."

"Actually, it was eight, but the eighth uprising spilled over into the **Ukrainian revolution of 1648–1676**."

"What did they demand?" Aliye asked, showing some interest in their conversation.

"All kinds of things. At first, the Cossacks wanted the gentry to register them and pay them for military service. Later, they demanded that they be granted 'knighthoods' to become equal with the nobility. The townspeople wanted towns to become independent of the feudal lords. The peasants also craved independence – personal this time. The gentry, for the most part, did not want any changes. Instead of negotiating, they crushed the uprisings. They believed, of course, that they were maintaining peace and stability in the country this way, but in fact, the Cossacks got so angry they signed an agreement with the Crimean Khanate and organized another uprising. This one was really huge. Peasants and townspeople, each with their own demands, joined them."

BOHDAN KHMELNYTSKYI

PETRO DOROSHENKO

IVAN BOHUN

"They signed an agreement with the Crimean Khanate for a good reason," Aliye added. "**In the early seventeenth century, the Cossacks helped the Crimean Khanate rebel against the Ottoman Empire**."

"In the end, **the Cossacks founded their own state**, the Hetmanate, and became its nobility and rulers," Yasia said. "There were many other twists and turns – civil wars in the Hetmanate and wars with neighbours who didn't want to recognize it. At the time, if a country wanted others to recognize it, it needed to have a king from an old dynasty, and the Hetmanate had trouble with that. So, they had to look for another country whose ruler would be willing to sign an agreement with them. They also persecuted Catholics and Uniates and banned Jews from settling down in the Hetmanate."

"What did Jews do wrong?"

"It's just that they were different," Aliye snapped. "And they didn't want to become like everyone else, because they'd have lost their identity. What's more, they didn't have their own country to protect them."

"That's right," Yasia said, rubbing her face. "There's another reason, too. The laws of the Polish–Lithuanian Commonwealth often turned Jews and the Orthodox into enemies – each of them could earn money only when the other one could not. The gentry often didn't want to collect taxes from the dependent peasants by themselves and recruited Jews to do it. The taxes were high. So, there you go. Revolution. Chaos. The gentry was far away and armed, while Jews were nearby and had no weapons."

"Sounds anything but heroic," Sashko said, shaking his head. "I thought that Cossacks were noble knights who defended our lands.

KYIV

THE HETMANATE

SICH (BEFORE 1652)

SICH (AFTER 1652)

But it turns out they were…"

"What? Just like their contemporaries?" interrupted Dmytryk, finishing his sentence for him. "I read a bit about Europe in the seventeenth century, and it was all the same: religious wars, plundering raids, revolutions and Jewish pogroms. But they did quite a lot of heroic and knightly things, too."

Sashko nodded.

"You're right," he said. "We can't judge our ancestors, because we're living in different times."

Dmytryk shook his head.

"No. I think we can. We *must* judge them, actually, as we are their descendants. But we can forgive them for not being better than their times."

8

8 TO REMEMBER WHO YOU ARE AND SURVIVE

"I need to talk to you, honey."

Sashko's mother was twisting a handkerchief in her hands, biting her lip.

"I need to go home for a few days. The checkpoints have reopened. Your grandpa is sick, and I'm worried about him. You will stay with Yulia until I come back, okay? You have stayed with her before."

"I want to go with you," Sashko said, knitting his brows. "I'm worried, too. Grandpa hasn't called for a while."

"No way. It's dangerous! I don't want you getting shot!"

Sashko felt as if something exploded in his chest.

"Then don't call that place home!" he shouted. "I don't even remember it! And I can't go there! I live here! This is my home!"

His mother burst out crying. Sashko slammed the door of his room and threw a pillow at the wall. He felt embarrassed and hurt at the same time. It was painful to remember his home – it'd been long six years since he visited it last. Sometimes, it seemed that it would be easier for both of them if his mother stopped holding on to Makiyivka and their relatives behind the frontline.

"Sweetheart," his mother said, knocking on the door of his room half an hour later. "Can we talk, please? I know that you're used to calling Zaporizhzhia your home. And I do realize you might not even remember our old flat and town. But you know, we moved away from Makiyivka for a reason. And it's also the reason we can't just go back. To stop calling the occupied territories our home means we'd have to accept the fact that they've been taken away from us. But it doesn't mean that you have to live there. And you don't even have to love the town you no longer remember. But we mustn't forget that it's our home – and we must remember who seized it from us. Then maybe one day we'll be able to claim this territory back. Do you understand what I'm saying?"

"I do," Sashko said, wiping away his tears before his mother noticed them. "But it's so hard…"

"I know, dear. But we can handle it. Together."

IVAN MAZEPA

RUSSIAN EMPIRE

VOLYN PROVINCE

CHERNIHIV

ZHYTOMYR

KYIV

LVIV

LITTLE RUSSIAN PROVINCE

KHARKIV

SLOBODA UKRAINE PROVINCE

AUSTRIAN EMPIRE

KAMYANETS-PODILSK

PODILLIA PROVINCE

NOVOROSIYSK

NOVOROSSIYA PROVINCE

OTTOMAN EMPIRE

"So, what's on our agenda today?" Sashko asked matter-of-factly.

"**The Crimean Khanate** losing its independence," Aliye said.

"And the Hetmanate gaining it," Yasia added. "And all of it because of the Russian Empire."

"Well, it was called the Tsardom of Muscovy back then," Dmytryk said, correcting her. "**The Hetmanate made an alliance with it because the rulers decided it was safer than an agreement with Poland or the Ottoman Empire**. At first, the Tsardom of Muscovy tried to bind the Hetmanate to them through unfair agreements with hetmans. Some of the hetmans were okay with that, but others, like Ivan Mazepa, tried to sign a treaty with the king of some other country, as they suspected that cooperation with Muscovy would never benefit Ukraine.

"After Mazepa died in 1709, the Tsardom of Muscovy was transformed into the Russian Empire in 1721. And the empire didn't want any of its parts to keep the self-government rights the Hetmanate had.

"But **Mazepa's ally, Charles XII of Sweden, lost the Great Northern War, and its winner, Russian emperor Peter the Great, destroyed the town of Baturyn, the seat of Mazepa, along with thousands of the townspeople, and reduced the position of the hetmans**. He also ordered Zaporizhzhia Sich be destroyed and sent tens of thousands of Ukrainians away to the north of the Russian Empire to build its new capital, Saint Petersburg.

"**After Peter the Great died, the Cossack leaders gradually restored most of the Hetmanate's rights and liberties**. They planned court intrigues, played tricks and made temporary agreements. Finally, they calmed down, confident that they would always be able to defend their country and their rights and liberties set forth in the agreement with the Russian Empire. Let the empire live in whatever way it likes, they thought.

"However, the Russian Empire was not going to stick to the agreement."

Sashko nodded.

"Right," he said. "When the empire grew strong enough, and **Empress Catherine the Great came to power, she started to erase any traces of self-government in the territories the empire claimed, the lands of the Hetmanate included. Catherine the Great destroyed Zaporizhzhia Sich again – this time forever.**"

"**She also annexed the Crimean Khanate in 1783,**" Aliye said with a bitter sigh.

"The Russian Empire craved as much access to the sea as possible," Sashko said, spreading his arms. "And as much land as possible. **The conquest of Crimea ruined the Cossacks and strangled the Hetmanate**: the Wild Fields did not exist anymore, and the Sich could not be reborn again, **as had happened after the death of Peter the Great**. And then afterward, with the war with the Ottoman Empire still going on, **Catherine the Great struck a deal with the rulers of two other empires, German and Austrian, and they split the Polish–Lithuanian Commonwealth between them**. So, the west of Ukraine went over to Austria and the rest of it to the Russian Empire, and Poland was divided into 'three unequal halves,' as Poles say."

"What about the Cossack leaders?" Dmytryk wondered, looking sullen. "Didn't they even try to do anything about it? To save their country?"

Sashko only shook his head. Yasia jumped in.

"Some of them tried to, but there were too few of them, and the Russian Empire was too powerful.

POLITICAL SYSTEM OF THE HETMANATE

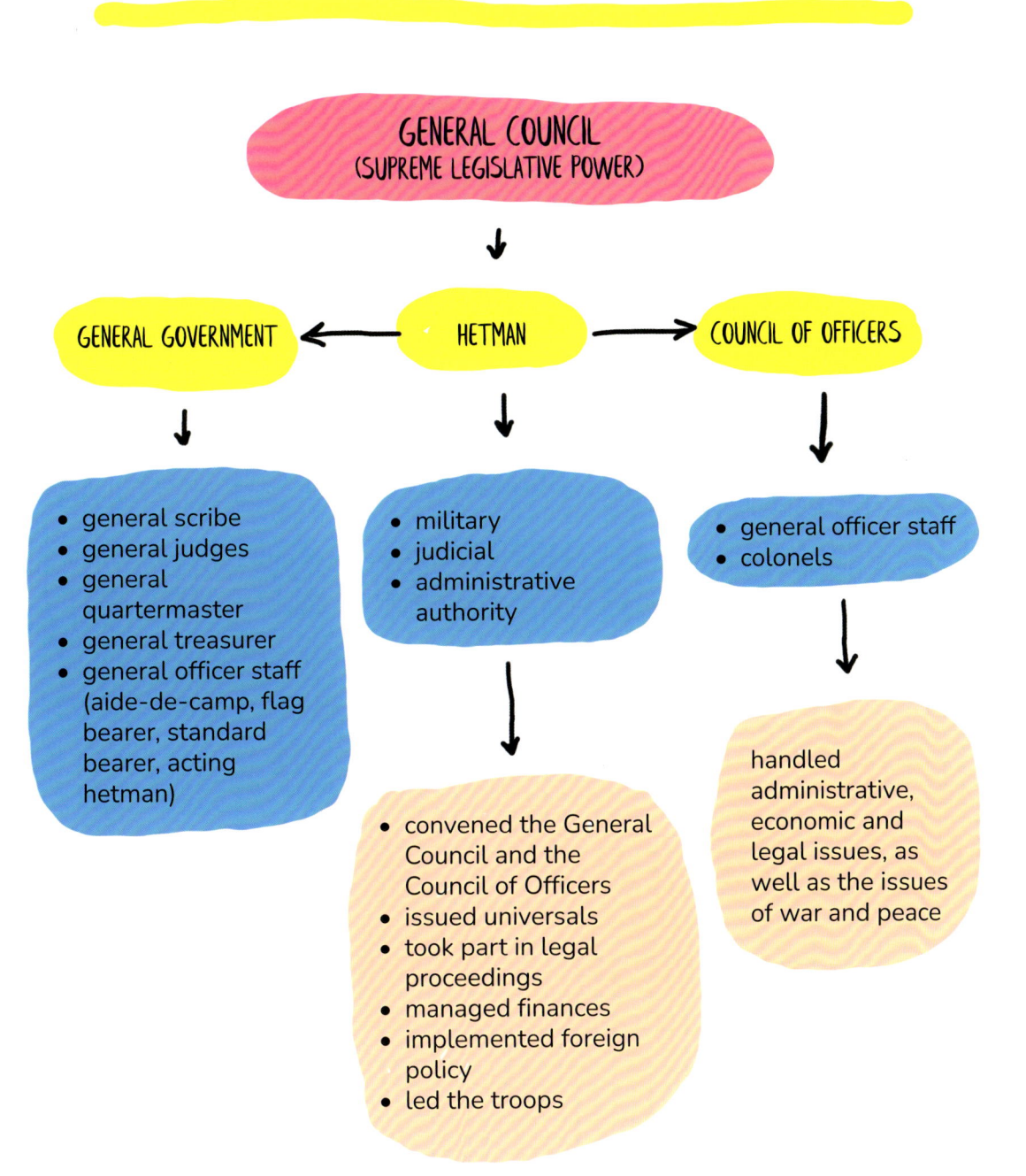

GENERAL COUNCIL
(SUPREME LEGISLATIVE POWER)

↓

GENERAL GOVERNMENT ← **HETMAN** → **COUNCIL OF OFFICERS**

General Government:
- general scribe
- general judges
- general quartermaster
- general treasurer
- general officer staff (aide-de-camp, flag bearer, standard bearer, acting hetman)

Hetman:
- military
- judicial
- administrative authority

- convened the General Council and the Council of Officers
- issued universals
- took part in legal proceedings
- managed finances
- implemented foreign policy
- led the troops

Council of Officers:
- general officer staff
- colonels

handled administrative, economic and legal issues, as well as the issues of war and peace

'THE AENEID'

•••••••••

••••• ,

—•—•—

BY VIRGIL

••••

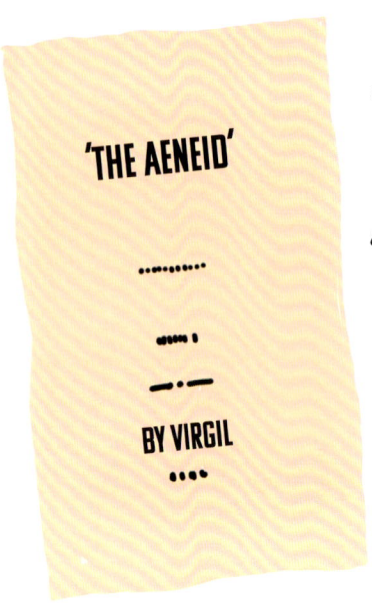

'ENEIDA' BY IVAN KOTLIAREVSKYI

The Russian Empire was clever. They granted land plots and privileges to the Cossack seniors. And then they turned all of them into slave owners."

"How?"

Everyone stared at Yasia.

"The Russian Empire introduced serfdom to Ukraine."

"I'm not surprised," Aliye said, wrinkling her nose. "It existed in the Austrian Empire, too."

Yasia shook her head.

"It was different," she said.

"Serfdom had existed in these lands ever since the Kyivan Rus. But the peasants only had to pay or work off the dues they owed to the landlord for using their land. And they didn't have much freedom of movement – only on special days throughout the year. But Russian serfdom was, in fact, slavery. The feudal lords could sell their serfs and take away their children. And people had no right to move anywhere or take their landowner to court …** they had no rights whatsoever!

"And so it happened that the Cossack seniors were granted powers like that over the Ukrainian peasants. They were given a chance to 'prove their loyalty' to the empire. They were promised money, success and the highest offices – up to that of a chancellor, who was like the present-day prime minister! To get all that, they had to do only one little thing – forget that they were Ukrainians. Not even that: they could remember their country as a 'picturesque nook of the empire'. But not as a country that was once independent and could regain its independence."

The children fell silent.

"So what happened then?" Aliye asked, breaking the silence. "Did all of them forget about Ukraine for good?"

"Everyone thought so. And then a soldier from the Poltava region, Ivan Kotliarevskyi, wrote a humorous poem, *Eneida*. It was a remake of another old poem dating back to the times of the Roman Empire: *The Aeniad* by Virgil. But it was written in Ukrainian. **That was how modern Ukrainian literature was born**. In fact, the poem was **about the Hetmanate, the destroyed Sich and the hopes that Ukraine would be reborn**. The author only seemed to be joking.

TARAS SHEVCHENKO

"*Eneida* was extremely popular. And it did remind some people about Ukraine. Things like that were also happening in the west of Ukraine, where, instead of Kotliarevskyi, they had three young men that called themselves 'The Ruthenian Triad'. Austrian officials were indignant, as they believed that the trio was trying '**to resurrect … the dead Ruthenian nationality**'."

"And did they really resurrect it?"

"Well, we are sitting here, aren't we?" Yasia said, laughing. "Then Taras Shevchenko appeared. He was a serf. A few Ukrainian artists bought him out of serfdom for his incredible talent for painting and poetry. Shevchenko appealed to many, if not everyone. And for that … or, actually, not only for that, he was exiled to Kazakhstan.

"When I was reading about the nineteenth century, I saw so many names of poets and writers: Ivan Franko, Lesia Ukrainka, Olha Kobylianska and many, many others in both parts of Ukraine. The abolition of serfdom was also mentioned, but mostly it was all about writers. It seemed that the most important mission for Ukrainians in that century was to remember who they were and not get lost in the empire. Perhaps, not only for Ukrainians."

LESIA UKRAINKA --→

IVAN FRANKO

"But what about serfdom?"

Yasia tapped on her phone and read out loud:

"During the war with the Ottoman empire in 1855…"

"What? Another war?" the children asked in unison.

"And it wasn't even the last one! So, Russia was losing that war, and in the Kyiv and Chernihiv provinces, **a manifesto was published calling people to sign up as volunteers**. The peasants decided that volunteer fighters clearly meant Cossacks. And Cossacks were free. The whole villages took the Cossack oath and declared that they'd no longer work off their dues and obey the landlords. What's more, they refused to obey the local officials, as the Cossacks had a self-government. The authorities had a hard time trying to put down that riot – the Kyiv Cossackdom. And then they lost the war, as it turned out that even though the empire could survive with slavery, it lacked the money and fighting spirit to win. In the end, they decided to make changes, abolish serfdom and introduce the *zemstvo* reform…"

"What's that?"

"Dad explained that it was a kind of decentralization. But it was distorted and incomplete. They also introduced education and land reforms. Things got better, but not for long."

99

9

9 PARENTS AND CHILDREN OF THE FIRST UKRAINIAN WAR OF INDEPENDENCE

Dmytryk knew a secret sign: if his mother had a day off, they should expect a visit from strangers in military uniform. This time was no exception, only the visitor was not a stranger. Bohdana from Uzhhorod, who was now drinking tea with his mother in the kitchen, was an old family friend.

"Oh dear! Is that Dmytryk?" Bohdana cried out, clasping her hands.

Mother laughed.

"I don't think I have any other sons."

"What a big boy! You'll be taller than me by the time I see you next year. Will you join us, honey? I'd love to hear how you've been doing."

Dmytryk nodded eagerly. He wasn't all that interested in talking with the visitor but wanted to spend every moment with his mum.

"… So we were trying to figure out **where they sent Shevchenko to after his first arrest**. To Kazakhstan or Turkestan…"

"He was sent to the Orsk Fortress **on the present-day border between Russia and Kazakhstan**," Bohdana said.

"Are you sure?" Dmytryk asked, wrinkling his brow.

"Yes. Those Turkestan rifle regiments where Shevchenko was sent were later reorganized many times until my 128th Mountain

ORSK FORTRESS

KAZAKHSTAN

TURKESTAN

THE BANNER OF THE UKRAINIAN SICH RIFLEMEN

Assault Brigade was formed. Fortunately, it's in Ukraine, not in some part of the Russian Empire."

"Oh wow. I can only imagine how many times it's been shaken up…"

"I know," Bohdana said. "The twentieth century was really good at shaking things up."

When they all logged in to chat, a strange image on the blue background appeared instead of Dmytryk's face.

"What's that?" Sashko asked.

"It's the flag of the Ukrainian Sich Riflemen. We studied their songs in school."

"We did, too!" Aliye said with excitement. "I also recited our anthem, 'Ant etkenmen'!"

"So, your classmates no longer pester you, do they?" Yasia asked with caution.

"No. The teachers and their parents had a long and tedious conversation with them. But," Aliye said, frowning, "it doesn't mean that I forgave them! Anyways, this is not what we're supposed be talking about."

"Right," Sashko agreed. "We had planned to discuss the reforms in the Russian Empire. They were far from perfect but worked anyway. The Austro-Hungarian Empire introduced them even earlier. **All kinds of businesses started to open in Ukraine, and their owners earned good money**. These people, the middle class, considered themselves Ukrainians. Perhaps they didn't think much about independence but they supported research and culture. They knew other Ukrainians beyond the imperial borders and set up the first political parties to protect their rights. Back in the day, it was not easy to publish books or stage a play in Ukrainian. **The Russian Empire issued a few orders that banned people from publishing books in the Ukrainian language**. They even banned their import later, as people started to print books in the west of Ukraine and ship them across the border. It was even forbidden to use Ukrainian as the language of instruction in elementary schools!

"**In 1905**, a revolution broke out in the Russian Empire. **The emperor was forced to sign the manifesto of 17 October that abolished all those orders for all the peoples of the Russian Empire**."

"But...?" Yasia asked with suspicion.

"But **in 1914**, the First World War hit," Dmytryk said. "You see, big empires had divided the world between them by that point. Each of them couldn't get enough, though – they wanted more and more territories. So the empires created alliances and started to fight with each other."

"The Austro-Hungarian Empire – yes, it was no longer just Austrian – approved the creation of national volunteer units in its army. That's how the legion of Ukrainian Sich Riflemen appeared."

"Why did they volunteer to fight in someone else's war?" Sashko asked, pulling a face. "Especially knowing that there were Ukrainians behind the frontline, too?"

"To learn how to fight. No empire was going to recognize Ukraine's independence just like that!"

"By the way, the legion of Ukrainian Sich Riflemen had a women's squad!" Yasia added. "Olena Stepaniv was its commander. And it was at the time when women were expected to stay at home and obey their father and husband, steering clear of politics, let alone war!"

"Some idiots still think so," Dmytryk said. Now it was his turn to pull a face. "Mama bumps into them all the time.

"Russia pulled out of the war in 1917, after another revolution exploded. The oppressed nations used this opportunity and launched their own revolutions. On 4 March 1917, the Ukrainian Central Council was established in Kyiv, headed by Mykhailo Hrushevskyi. A bit later, in June, the Central Council announced the autonomy of the Ukrainian People's Republic within the Russian Empire. And what was happening in Crimea, Aliye?"

"**The Crimean People's Republic was proclaimed**. It happened a bit later, in December 1917. We were the first Muslims to proclaim a republic – as well as the first Muslims to recognize the right of all women to vote."

"And you did it only four years after a non-Muslim country did that for the first time in history," Yasia said. "What did the Crimean People's Republic do afterward?"

Aliye clenched her teeth and took a deep breath.

"Nothing. They managed to elect the government and the parliament, but a few weeks later, the Bolsheviks overthrew them."

The children fell silent. In that

period, Ukraine had held out for only a few years. But a few years was much longer than two weeks.

"The Bolsheviks? Who were they?" Sashko asked, switching topics.

Yasia gladly picked it up.

"They were **members of the Russian Communist Party**. At that time, a civil war was raging in Russia between the right and left, and **the communists**. Dad says there were democrats among them, too, but they were quickly silenced. You know how the communists are … **They believed they could get rid of injustice in the world by getting rid of private property**. When everything is shared, and everyone gets only as much as they need, injustice will not exist. That's what they thought."

Dmytryk protested.

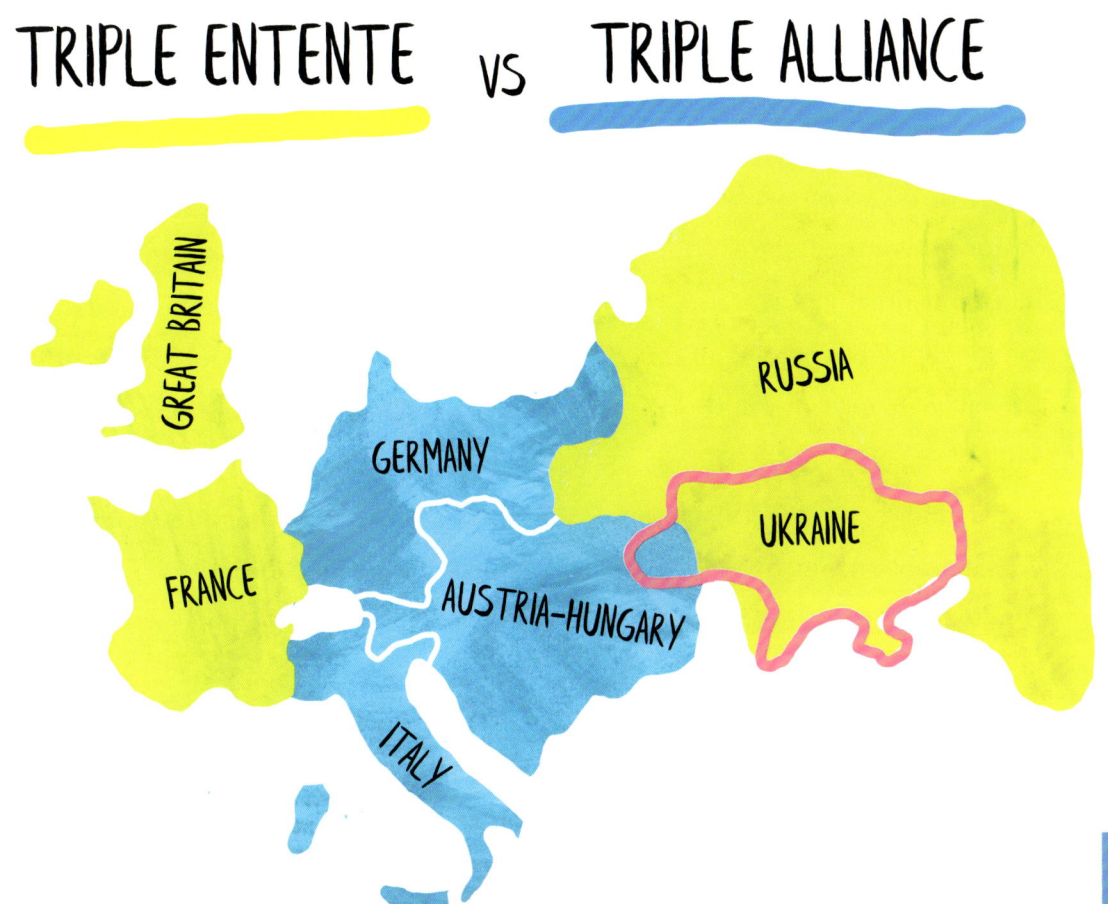

TRIPLE ENTENTE vs TRIPLE ALLIANCE

GREAT BRITAIN
FRANCE
GERMANY
AUSTRIA-HUNGARY
ITALY
RUSSIA
UKRAINE

107

"But some things must be private! Some keepsakes. Presents. A toothbrush, at least! How were they planning to go about it?"

"I don't think they ever thought about presents or toothbrushes," Yasia said. "**They thought only about putting the Russian Empire back together and bringing communism to all its peoples. And if anyone disagreed with that, the communists simply planned to kill them – as the enemies of a bright future**. Actually, they killed them as soon as they conquered new territories. So, when the Bolsheviks took over Kyiv, the Central Council signed an agreement with the German Empire to help it get rid of them. In its turn, the Ukrainian People's Republic, or the UPR, promised to feed the German army.

This problem was fixed, but there were so many others. The UPR badly needed reforms, but different people imagined them differently. Finally, **on 29 April 1918**, a coup was staged. Instead of the UPR, **the Ukrainian State was proclaimed**, headed by hetman Pavlo Skoropadskyi. Yet, **on 13 November 1918**, Skoropadskyi was overthrown, and **the UPR Directorate was proclaimed**. It meant that the country was ruled by several people, members of the Directorate, whose leaders were Volodymyr Vynnychenko and Symon Petliura.

Meanwhile, the Central Powers lost the war. The Austro-Hungarian Empire collapsed, and **in October 1918**, the Western Ukrainian National Republic was established. **Immediately, it had to fight with the newly established Poland**, as Poles claimed the WUPR's lands as their own. **In January 1919, the WUPR and the UPR united into one state** – that's why we celebrate Unity Day on 22 January.

Still, they couldn't help each

UKRAINIAN PEOPLE'S REPUBLIC

AUTONOMY

CRIMEAN PEOPLE'S REPUBLIC

MYKHAILO HRUSHEVSKYI ---> **CENTRAL COUNCIL**

other that much. In February 1919, the Bolsheviks were advancing toward Kyiv. Poles had already conquered Lviv in November 1918. The winners of the First World War, the Allies, were supporting both Poles and Russians."

"Which Russians?" Aliye wondered. "The Bolsheviks or the whites?"

"The whites," Yasia said. "They supported them so fervently that when the 1919 typhus epidemic broke out in the Ukrainian army,

France blocked all the attempts of the Directorate to buy medicine. They wanted the Russian Empire to revive. They didn't want to deal with some new country they'd have to negotiate with.

So, fast-forward through all the incredible feats and horrible tragedies, and we see that **in 1921, the Bolsheviks conquered the UPR, and in the summer of 1919, Poland occupied the WUPR**. Both governments went into exile. The First Ukrainian War of Independence was over."

"So, their efforts were wasted?" Sashko asked in a miserable voice.

"Not at all," Yasia said, shaking her head. "They did a whole lot. **They had just enough time to make Ukrainian the language of instruction in schools and set up Ukraine's Academy of Sciences in 1918. They made themselves known in the world**, even if the world didn't want to hear about them. The children who studied in Ukrainian schools grew up as the generation of artists of the 1920s: writers, poets, sculptors, painters, playwrights and many, many others ... Those few years of independence

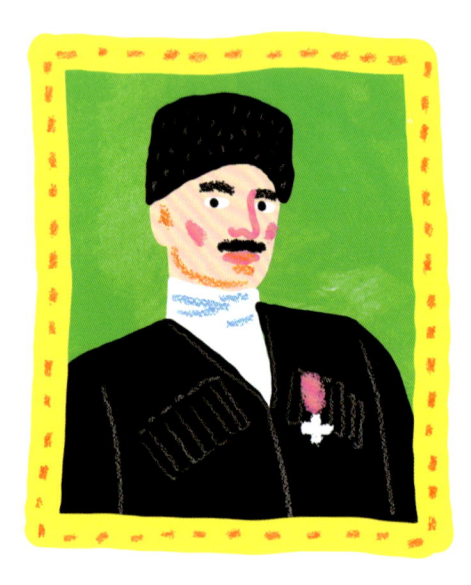

PAVLO SKOROPADSKYI

awakened such a power that even the Bolsheviks could not crush it and had to play along with it, at least for some time. I think they did so much during those few years that their efforts weren't wasted!"

VOLODYMYR VYNNYCHENKO

SYMON PETLIURA

DIRECTORATE

29 APRIL 1918

13 NOVEMBER 1918

WUPR

UKRAINIAN STATE

111

10

10 ATTEMPTS TO TURN THE TIDE

"I need to talk to you," Yasia said gravely. Her father got up and put his hand around her shoulders.

"Sure. What are you worried about?"

"Well … you know…" she mumbled, embarrassed about her thoughts. "I just can't stop thinking about the Ukrainian People's Republic. Could they have done anything differently? Perhaps they wouldn't have died so soon… Or wouldn't have died at all!"

"You know, Yasia," her father said, sitting down on the floor next to the sofa. "I've thought long and hard about it, too. And I do believe they did their best."

"But they fought with each other!"

"Right. And played into coups, too," her father nodded. "And wasted time. And made mistakes – just like any people. But if countries lost their independence only for that reason, there wouldn't be any independent states left in the world. It happens like that sometimes: you do whatever you can but it's simply not enough."

Yasia took off her glasses and turned them in her hands, confused.

"I'm scared even to think about it. If there're things you can't change no matter how hard you try, does that mean Russians can conquer us again now?"

"I'm afraid we forgot to tell you that you're too young for these

THEN

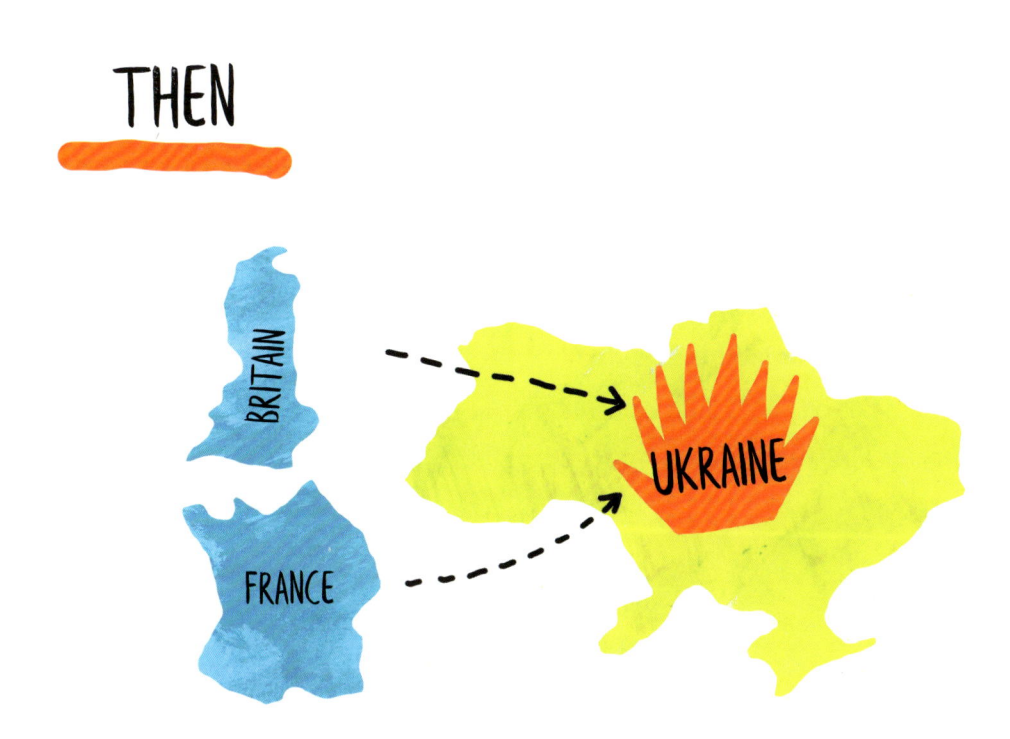

BRITAIN → UKRAINE

FRANCE → UKRAINE

NOW

BRITAIN, UKRAINE, FRANCE

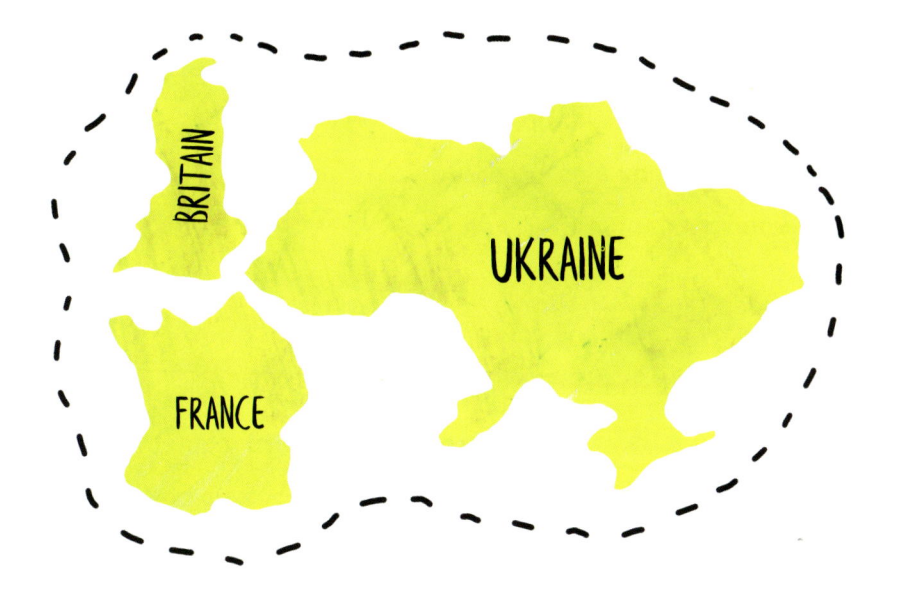

questions," her father said with a sad smile. "Yes, they can. But on the other hand, the world has changed. **And the Allies that didn't want to see the UPR on the world map have been on our side ever since the war started**. We could count it as one of our achievements, don't you think?"

"Why all these dull faces?" Dmytryk asked, even though his face was just as dull.

"We're allergic to the twentieth century," Sashko said. "Let's get started."

"Okay," Aliye said with a nod. "**In 1921, the Bolsheviks occupied the whole of Crimea and annexed it to Russia. They also occupied Ukraine**, renaming it the Ukrainian Soviet Socialist Republic, or the SSR. In the same year, many countries occupied by the Bolsheviks suffered from hunger – the occupiers made sure to take away all the food people had. Foreign aid helped deal with hunger, though. And then, in 1921, the Bolsheviks decided to give the Soviet Union countries, exhausted by war, a breath of fresh air: they allowed people to set up small private companies and supported the national cultures. This policy was called nativization, and in Ukraine, 'Ukrainization'."

"It looked like the Bolsheviks were scared of the consequences of their own policies and relaxed them. But it was just an impression. Very soon, **in 1928, the New Economic Policy was cancelled**, and all these liberties were taken away. **The peasants were ordered to unite into collective farms – large shared enterprises. They had to give all their lands and cattle over to those farms**. 'The peasants have become too brazen,' the Bolsheviks thought. 'How dare they think they're their own masters!'"

Yasia gave her a crooked smile.

Map labels: POLAND, CZECHOSLOVAKIA, SOVIET UNION, UKRAINIAN SSR, CRIMEAN SSR

"But the peasants did not agree to that," Aliye continued. "They organized riots when the Bolsheviks pressurized them. Then the authorities remembered their tried-and-tested weapon – hunger. They locked the peasants down in their villages and **introduced passports for townspeople**. The peasants were assigned to particular collective farms and had to stay put – it was illegal for them to move elsewhere. **And then the Bolsheviks hit them with famine. In the autumn of 1932**, they seized the entire harvest. Didn't even leave them any grain for seeding. They also snatched all the food people kept in their pantries, condemning millions of peasants to death by starvation. It's called genocide – **intentional destruction of a group of people**. Those who considered themselves Ukrainians died of hunger. And the survivors no longer rebelled or mentioned that they were Ukrainians."

"They didn't mention it for some time," Sashko remarked. "And what was happening in Western Ukraine? Was life there any better there than in the Soviet Union?"

"Anywhere in the world was better than in the Soviet Union," Dmytryk said, shaking his head. "But they did have their own troubles. Poles didn't like it, either, that Ukrainians wanted to have a state of their own. They firmly believed that Western Ukraine belonged to them. **Zakarpattia (usually referred to as Transcarpathia) was the luckiest: it became part of democratic Czechoslovakia and had its own government**.

"Meanwhile, two other milestone events happened: **the associations of Ukrainian students and youth, active mostly in Poland, gathered together in Vienna in 1929 and united into the Organization of Ukrainian Nationalists**. Yevhen Konovalets, a veteran of the legion of the Ukrainian Sich Riflemen, was elected as its head. In 1932, the Nazi party gained majority votes in an election in Germany. Its leader, Adolf Hitler, became the chancellor (elected head of the government) a year after that and **promised Germans revenge for their country's bitter, heavy defeat in the First World War**.

"The activists of the Organization of Ukrainian Nationalists knew that Ukraine had collaborated with Germany and hoped to renew collaboration, as Germany was rising again after its defeat."

"It was a bad idea," Yasia said, wincing. "And not only because Hitler destroyed all his political opponents or blamed Jews for all of Germany's problems and persecuted them. In fact, they didn't have any

HEAD

YEVHEN KONOVALETS

ORGANIZATION OF UKRAINIAN NATIONALISTS

EMBLEM

BANNER

AVHUSTYN VOLOSHYN

idea at the time that Hitler would organize a genocide. It's just that he had concluded agreements with the Soviet Union. And then there was Carpathian Ukraine.

"In 1938, Hitler occupied part of the Czechoslovakian territories. He claimed that Czechoslovakia was violating the rights of Germans living there and he was the one to protect them. Next spring, Hitler literally gifted Carpathian Ukraine, as Zakarpattia was called then, to Hungary.

"The Czechoslovakian army retreated from Zakarpattia, and the Hungarian troops entered. Avhustyn Voloshyn, a priest and prime minister from Carpathian Ukraine, tried to outplay Hitler on the diplomatic front and asked Germany to declare a protectorate over Carpathian Ukraine. Hitler had been playing the role of peacekeeper, and Voloshyn expected he'd either agree to that or throw off his mask. Unfortunately, Hitler chose the latter. And Voloshyn and other Ukrainians in Zakarpattia chose to fight..."

"And?!" cried out three voices in Yasia's headphones.

"The miracle never happened," Yasia said with a sad smile. "But they didn't surrender. **That was how the Second World War started for Ukraine. For all others, it started in six months.**"

"In general, the leaders of the Organization of Ukrainian Nationalists realized that **the Nazis should not be trusted**," Dmytryk said. "At least, most of them. **Back in 1938**, they quarreled over it and split into two factions: the OUN-M led by Andriy Melnyk – Konovalets had been killed earlier by the Soviet security services – and the OUN-B led by Stepan Bandera. Bandera's supporters did not trust Germans but collaborated with them. Few countries in Europe wanted to go to war with the Soviet Union.

"But most of all, everyone hoped that the Soviet Union and Germany would exhaust themselves with a long war: then Ukraine would fight both of them back, they hoped, and declare independence. **When the Second World War broke out, both factions of the Organization of Ukrainian Nationalists sent expeditionary groups into Central Ukraine and started to build an underground network**.

"However, the longer the two factions collaborated with the Nazis, the clearer they saw the similarities between the Nazis and the Bolsheviks. **The Bolsheviks wanted to destroy 'the enemies of the world's communist revolution', while the Nazis were after the people and nations they considered second-rate**. Both the Nazis and the Bolsheviks didn't have enough prisons, so they built concentration camps, keeping thousands of prisoners there in terrible conditions. Thousands of Ukrainians, who were predominantly Jewish, were locked in Nazi and Soviet camps.

"The OUN leaders realized that Ukraine had to get rid of its ally, as it wasn't any better than the Soviet Union. So, **on 30 June 1941,**

THE HUNGARIAN AND POLISH INVASION OF CARPATHIAN UKRAINE

POLAND

UKRAINIAN TROOPS

6 M 400 S

SLOVAKIA

CARPATHIAN UKRAINE

7 M 70 S   2 M 20 S   1 M 30 S   1 M 30 S   9 M 120 S   30 M 400 S

ROMANIA

HUNGARY

ENEMY TROOPS

M — MACHINE GUNS
S — SICH RIFLEMEN

in Lviv, Stepan Bandera, Yaroslav Stetsko and their supporters declared the restoration of Ukraine's independence. They were immediately sent to a concentration camp. They knew perfectly well that the Nazis would not recognize their declaration. All they wanted to do was to tell the world that **Ukraine was not collaborating with the Nazis. Ukraine was fighting for its own state**, even if it had to fight against both the Nazis and the Soviet Union.

"In a few months, the OUN faction headed by Melnyk followed the same route. Meanwhile in 1941, the Polissian Sich, **the Ukrainian People's Revolutionary Army**, was formed in the Polissia region.

122

It was the army of the Ukrainian People's Republic that also wanted to join the war and fight for Ukraine's independence. **Bandera's supporters established their own Ukrainian Insurgent Army in 1942**."

"Why did they act separately?" Aliye asked angrily. "Why didn't they come to an agreement and collaborate?"

Dmytryk threw up his hands and said:

"I think they wondered about that, too. But they just didn't have the space and time to strike a deal. The Second World War was raging. The leaders of all three organizations lived in different countries. They also argued for important reasons, as each of them imagined the fight, the future of Ukraine and the limits of what was acceptable in the war differently. You can't agree on these things quickly

MOVEMENT OF EXPEDITIONARY GROUPS AS OF SEPTEMBER 1941

BERDYCHIV BILA TSERKVA
UKRAINIAN EXPEDITIONARY GROUPS
THE EASTERN FRONT
ODESA
DZHANKOI

STEPAN BANDERA **YAROSLAV STETSKO**

INDEPENDENCE

30 JUNE 1941 → **LVIV**

and without arguments. It was really hard for them to unite. It's a shame, though, that they were fighting with each other, as if the enemies they had were not enough."

"Perhaps that's the reason they lost? They wasted their energy fighting with each other, didn't they?" Aliye asked.

"Or, perhaps, their enemies were too powerful, and one of them, the Soviet Union, was supported by the Allies. They condemned the Nazi crimes but turned a blind eye to those committed by the communists. **The Ukrainian Insurgent Army was holding out against the Soviet Union until the 1950s**, but the Allies agreed to recognize the Soviet Union's absolute power over all of Eastern Europe to avoid provoking a new war. They simply ignored the crimes committed by the Soviet Union."

Aliye sobbed and clenched her fists.

"The war was coming to an end in 1944 when Joseph Stalin, the Soviet Union's ruler, decided that my nation was standing in his way," she said. "And we're a small nation – twenty million or so. So, he blamed the *kırımlı* for collaborating with the Nazis and ordered their deportation from Crimea. In just three days, my whole nation was deported in cargo trains to Siberia and Central Asia. **Almost half of the people died during the deportation or in the first few years of the exile**. It was forbidden even to mention that our nation existed. Amet-khan Sultan, a **fighter pilot serving in the Soviet army, was twice awarded Hero of the Soviet Union, the highest title at the time**. After the deportation, the government wanted to grant him a third award, but they demanded that Amet-khan renounce his people first. He refused.

And no one – not a single person! – was sentenced for doing all that!"

"They *will* be sentenced," Yasia said. "We will sentence them."

AMET-KHAN SULTAN

11

11. HANDING OVER THE FLAG

MOTHER   **FATHER**   **DMYTRYK**

Sashko's mother returned the following week, just as she had promised.

"How was your trip?" Sashko asked. "How's grandpa?"

"He's alright," his mother said, hugging him. "Feeling better. I ... I also met with your father."

"Oh, really?" Sashko said, pulling a face. "So, his Russian relatives didn't quite welcome him, did they?"

"I guess not," mother said with a

half-smile. "He wants to meet you, too. Would you like to see him?"

"He left us," Sashko snapped. "Two years ago."

His mother sighed.

"Your father and I separated because I chose Ukraine, and he preferred Russia. But now he's back in Makiyivka. And he's still your father."

"It's not only you. I chose Ukraine, too," Sashko said. "And I don't think Dad and I have much to talk about."

"I hope we'll have a bit more fun today," Dmytryk said, scratching his nose.

"At least we're going to bury the Soviet Union," Sashko said. "Good riddance!"

Aliye protested.

"We'll bury Stalin first!" she said. "He died **in 1953**, and his successor, Nikita Khrushchev, stopped throwing people in concentration camps and shooting anyone who disagreed with government policy. Well, he didn't really stop it, but **the persecutions became less severe. The period under Khrushchev's rule is called the Thaw**."

"They just didn't have enough money for the shootings, did they?"

"Right. They didn't," Aliye said. "At that point, the dissident movement emerges. **Dissidents fought for human rights in the Soviet Union**. They were writers and poets, artists and human rights activists. They tried to take advantage of the Thaw and demanded protection for the Ukrainian language and culture, as well as creative freedom for themselves. The thing is that censorship agencies in the Soviet Union strictly regulated what you could or couldn't write, and the writers could be jailed for writing 'wrong' texts. So, the dissidents demanded reforms and called for stopping persecutions and protecting human rights. They could only dream of independence, since the Soviet

LEVKO LUKIANENKO

Union seemed too powerful back then. And the *kırımlı* dreamed of returning to Crimea."

"By the way, did the Soviets return Crimea to Ukraine?" Dmytryk wondered.

"They did in 1954. But it was ruined and devastated. The Soviet Union was not going to waste its money to restore it. And the Russians relocated there did not know how to farm in a drought-ridden steppe, so Ukraine was ordered to build a canal to supply water to Crimea."

"Some people were dreaming of more than independence," Dmytryk said, pulling up a photo onto his screen. "**In 1961, a group of lawyers headed by Levko Lukianenko ended up in court for setting up their own underground party: in the Soviet Union, all parties other than the Communist Party were forbidden. They planned to fight not only for civil rights and liberties, but also for Ukraine's independence**. Levko Lukianenko was sentenced to death for those plans, and his fellows to fifteen years in labor camps. Lukianenko spent almost three months on death row, and he woke up every morning thinking he'd be killed that day. But in the end, **he was sent to a labor camp instead**.

In the labor camps, the Ukrainian dissidents met the fighters of the Ukrainian Insurgent Army. As they joked, the warriors passed the baton of the fight for Ukraine to them."

VASYL STUS

Yasia rummaged through her notes.

"**In 1964, they plotted against Khrushchev, and Leonid Brezhnev came to power. He persecuted the dissidents much harder** and came up with an idea to lock them up not only in labor camps but in mental hospitals, too."

Sashko coughed.

"Did he mean that anyone who was against the Soviet Union was crazy?" he asked.

"Guess so," Yasia said. "But it was too late to stop their movement, even though it wasn't massive, and only some of its members spoke out against the Soviet Union. Meanwhile, the Soviet Union was destroying itself. **Nothing worked well, except for the persecutions**. Factories, collective farms, shops, schools, hospitals – nothing. **People didn't have money to buy food, clothes or basic toiletries**."

"But our neighbour, Russia, keeps claiming that people were kinder in the Soviet times," Dmytryk said, scratching the back of his head.

"They're lying!" Yasia snapped. "My grandpa says that people find it hard to realize what kind of nightmare they were living in. That's why they believe in fairy tales assuring them that everything was great in the past. Those who didn't want to live under constant pressure usually ended up in prison and died. Like that poet, Vasyl Stus."

Sashko perked up. "I heard about him. There's a book about his court case. His former attorney, Viktor Medvedchuk, filed a lawsuit against

131

THE UKRAINIAN STUDENT ASSOCIATION GOES ON HUNGER STRIKE

its authors, who said he hadn't even tried to defend Stus."

"What a fool," Dmytryk said, shaking his head. "But let's go back to the Soviet Union. What happened to it?"

"It started to collapse," Yasia said. "The government allowed the establishment of other political parties, and in 1989, Rukh, or the People's Movement of Ukraine, emerged. They didn't have that many supporters and weren't taken seriously, but **when they decided to celebrate the unity of the Ukrainian People's Republic and the West Ukrainian People's Republic by organizing a human chain from Lviv to Kyiv in 1990, they gathered a lot of momentum**. They even got enough votes at the parliamentary elections to win seats in the SSR's Verkhovna Rada. Just a few seats. But still, it was very important.

"Then the Kremlin decided to propose an updated union treaty with all the republics to save the Soviet Union. And then," Yasia said, smiling from ear to ear, "my grandpa came on stage."

"Your grandpa?"

"He was one of the students who organized the Revolution on Granite. In 1990, they went on hunger strike in downtown Kyiv for two weeks, demanding that the new union treaty should not be signed. And they succeeded: the Verkhovna Rada of the SSR refused to do it."

"Hmm," Sashko said. "I read that most countries in the world did not want the Soviet Union to collapse and tried to save it. Just as the Allies tried to save the Russian Empire.

George Bush, president of the United States, even arrived in Kyiv to ask Ukraine to keep a low profile: 'A war will break out as soon as you proclaim independence,' he said."

"I'm glad they didn't listen to him," Aliye said. "Otherwise, the Crimean Tatars would've never returned home."

"Oh! Look what I found!" Dmytryk exclaimed, slamming his hand on the desk. "It turns out that **the Act of Declaration Independence of Ukraine** was written by the very same Levko Lukianenko! So, he achieved the goal of his underground party! **On 24 August 1991, Ukraine proclaimed independence. And later, the government of the Ukrainian People's Republic in exile triumphantly handed the state regalia to the first president of the independent Ukraine**.

"That was how a centuries-long fight for our own state came to an end," Yasia said, smiling. But then she shook her head. "No. The fight is not over."

ACT OF DECLARATION OF INDEPENDENCE OF UKRAINE

In view of the mortal danger threatening Ukraine in connection with the state coup in the USSR on 19 August 1991,
- Continuing the thousand-year tradition of state building in Ukraine,
- Proceeding from the right of a nation to self-determination in accordance with the Charter of the United Nations and other international legal documents, and
- Implementing the Declaration of State Sovereignty of Ukraine, the Verkhovna Rada of the Ukrainian Soviet Socialist Republic solemnly

DECLARES
THE INDEPENDENCE OF UKRAINE

and the creation of an independent Ukrainian state – UKRAINE.
The territory of Ukraine is indivisible and inviolable.
From this day forward, only the Constitution and laws of Ukraine are valid on the territory of Ukraine.
This act becomes effective at the moment of its approval.

VERKHOVNA RADA OF UKRAINE

24 August 1991

12

12 UNDER THE BLUE-AND-YELLOW FLAG

"How can we find anybody here?" Yasia asked, looking at Shevchenko Park in Kyiv, full of people and flags.

"We'll find her," Dmytryk said. "You found me, didn't you? Look! A Crimean Tatar flag with the *tamga*! Aliye might be there."

Aliye really was there with her parents. But where was Sashko?

"It's the first time this whole year that we've had a chance to meet. Only to get lost in the crowd!" Yasia whimpered.

"Just call him," Rustem said. "Tell him that you're waiting for him under the *tamga* by the monument to Taras Shevchenko."

"And while we are waiting … Mama!" Aliye said, tugging at her mother's sleeve.

"Yes, *kızım*?"

"We can't figure out when Russia invaded Ukraine for the first time. After independence was declared, I mean."

"Well, right then – after Ukraine became independent," Niyara, Aliye's mother, snorted. "**They tried to occupy Crimea back in 1992**. My family didn't return from Uzbekistan until 1997, of course, but **it was in 1990 that the first Crimean Tatars came back**, and they told us what had been going on back then. They fought over their loyalties – Ukraine and Russia argued over to whom the officers of the former Soviet Black Sea fleet should swear their

MONUMENT TO SHEVCHENKO

THE CRIMEAN TATAR FLAG

allegiance. Ukraine pulled part of the soldiers over to its side, while Russia, in its turn, pressurized the sailors. Then one of the crews rebelled, and their ship boldly left Crimea for Odesa. They wanted to show that they chose Ukraine and were not going to change their minds."

"Sashko!" Aliye cried, seeing her friend coming. She hugged him. "Go on, Mama."

"Then Crimea's president was elected. A candidate from the party called 'Russia' won. And Russia – the country this time – trained criminal gangs on the peninsula. They wanted to occupy Crimea with their help. But Ukrainian secret services pitted those gangsters against each other and thwarted their plan."

"Wow! And what happened next?" Dmytryk asked.

"The Orange Revolution in 2004, of course. Ukraine had a hard time dealing with the problems inherited from the Soviet Union, but we were doing a good job until 2004. **And then, in 2004, two candidates ran for president – Viktor Yanukovych and Viktor Yushchenko. The first one was Russia's protégé. The second one proved himself a savvy prime minister and head of the National Bank. He also believed that Ukraine should move away from Moscow, protect the Ukrainian language and develop Ukrainian culture, not be ashamed of it**. You weren't born yet, but I can tell you that when I was young, it was embarrassing to speak Ukrainian in Kyiv. People laughed at you if you did. **Our leader, Mustafa Cemilev, was then a deputy from 'Nasha Ukraina' (Our Ukraine), Viktor Yushchenko's political party**.

"It was Yushchenko who won the election, but it was rigged in favor of Yanukovych. So, Ukrainians protested in Independence Square in Kyiv, demanding a re-count. After that, Yushchenko was elected president."

"Why is that an 'orange' revolution?"

"It was the colour of 'Nasha Ukraina'. During the protests, Independence Square was full of it."

"Like it's now full of blue and yellow?"

"No, not that much," Niyara laughed. "That was merely the party's colour. Blue and yellow are our national colours, and today it's the Independence Day of Ukraine."

People kept lining up on Khreshchatyk. There were so many of them! But the March of the Defenders was about to start in only two hours. The children were sitting on a bench in the park, drinking lemonade.

"My mama will be marching together with other officers from Kropyvnytskyi!" Dmytryk said proudly.

"We'll be marching in the Crimean section. It's not military," Aliye said, chewing on her drinking straw. "Would you like to join us?"

"I'll ask my parents if I can," Yasia said. She was trying to get an ice cube out of her paper cup with a straw. "Why do you think people elected Yanukovych after Yushchenko? Even if Yushchenko was a bad president … It's weird to elect the one you'd earlier protested against."

"Mama says that people lost confidence," Dmytryk sighed.

"Hostile relations with Russia

brought many problems to Ukraine, so people thought, 'Perhaps we made a mistake? What if we elect a president favoured by Russia and live in peace with our neighbour?'"

"But Yanukovych decided that if Ukrainians were so willing to live in peace with Russia, they didn't really need to be independent," Yasia said, making a face. "He was pro-Russia and wanted to undermine Ukraine's independence, so he promised to sign an agreement with Russia that would have taken away Ukraine's independence. **That was when Ukrainians realized that independence was dearer to them than friendship with Russia**."

"But if the Orange Revolution was more or less peaceful, then the Revolution of Dignity in the winter of 2013 was nothing like that," Sashko said. He drank his lemonade up and threw the cup away in a waste bin. "By the way, the relatives of the Heavenly Hundred, the people killed in Independence Square on 20 February 1914 – on the Maidan – will come first in the March of the Defenders."

"Why is it called the 'Heavenly Hundred'?"

"**There were self-defense units on the Maidan, a hundred people each, protecting protesters from the riot police that were told to crack down on them**," Sashko explained. "In the last few battles, so many people were killed that a whole unit could have been formed out of them. That's why that newly created unit was called 'Heavenly Hundred'. And coming back to Yanukovych: he knew that we would never forgive him for killing so many people, so he fled to ask his master – the Russian dictator, Vladimir Putin – for help."

Hearing that, Aliye bit her lip.

"And that dictator decided to start the war in Crimea."

"How did that happen?" Yasia

asked quietly. "Do you remember anything?"

"I don't! **On 26 February 2014, the Russian army invaded Crimea. They occupied towns and sieged the Ukrainian military. Crimean Tatars brought food to the Ukrainian officers and tried to help them. Because we are citizens of Ukraine! And Ukraine is our country, too!** My parents helped Ukrainian servicemen as well. But Russia occupied Crimea anyway, and started to persecute the locals who supported Ukraine. One of Mama's friends was captured. After that my parents and I fled. But I … I was only two years old! I don't remember

ORANGE REVOLUTION

VIKTOR YUSHCHENKO VS VIKTOR YANUKOVYCH

YES! YUSHCHENKO

anything! I don't remember Crimea..." Aliye burst into tears. "Only tulips blooming in the steppe. My parents returned from exile to Crimea only to lose their home again. And I don't even remember it!"

"Don't cry, Aliye," Sashko said, squeezing her hand. "I'm from Makiyivka, but all I remember is tulips in the steppe too. But we will go

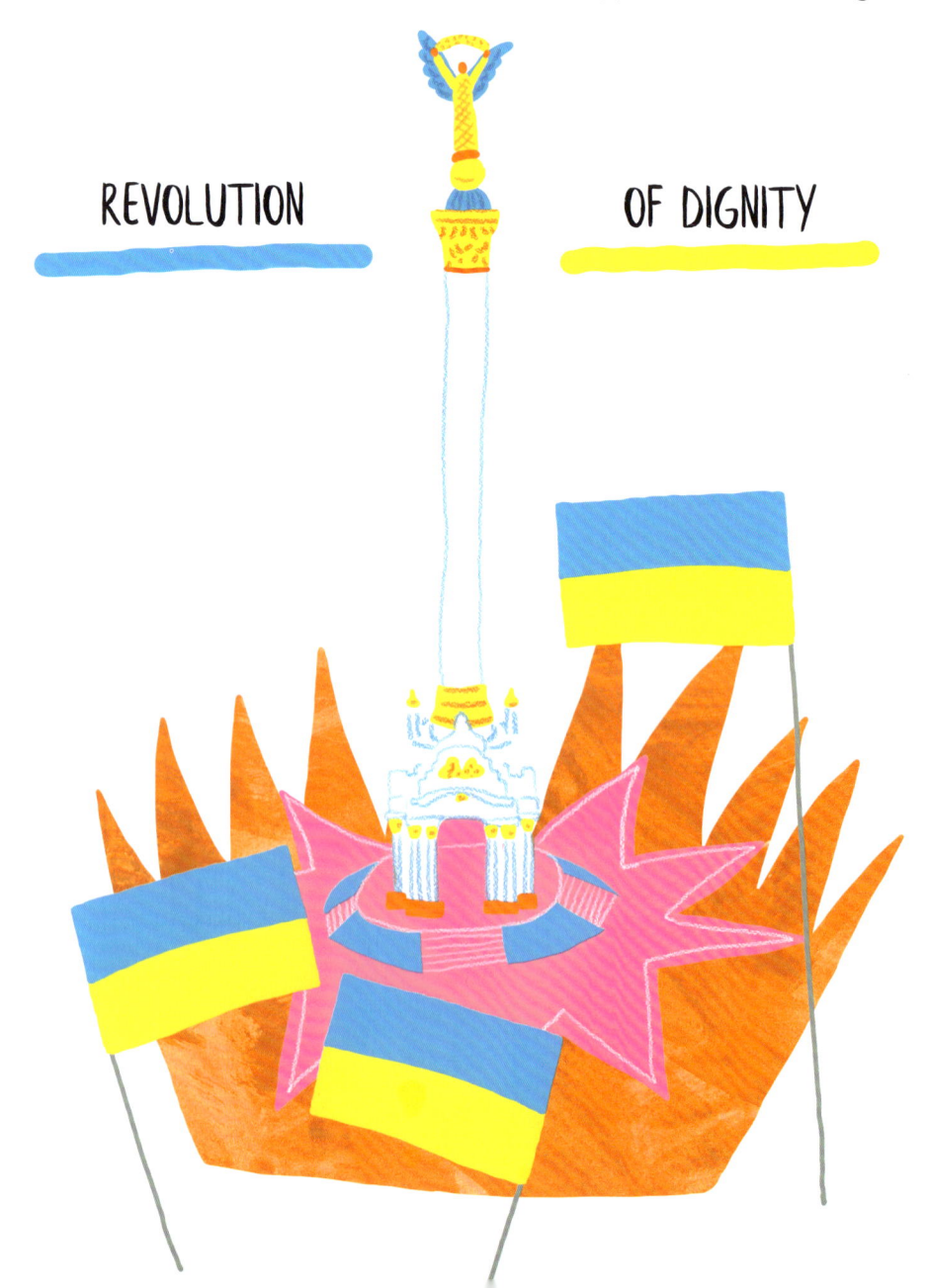

REVOLUTION OF DIGNITY

back! And you will return home, too, you'll see! I'll invite you over when the tulips bloom! I'll invite all of you! And then we'll visit you in Crimea!"

"Sure," Aliye sniffed. "But I'm so scared that it will never happen."

"Of course it will," Dmytryk said, trying to reassure her. "My mama will defeat them!"

"I will also join the military when I grow up," Yasia declared all of a sudden. "So, if your mother doesn't manage to beat them all up, I'll help her. Oh, look, the march is starting! Let's come closer!"

"You know what? I've been thinking..." Sashko said. "Our quest continues all the way to the present day, but we have to finish it somewhere, right? In some nice place."

"Do you have any ideas?" Yasia asked.

"I do," Sashko said, waving his hand towards the square full of people and flags. "Right here. At the March of the Defenders on the Independence Day of Ukraine."

SCYTHIAN

COSSACK

SOLDIER OF THE UKRAINIAN PEOPLE'S ARMY

DMYTRYK'S MOTHER

13

13. UKRAINE ON FIRE

It usually took more than twelve hours to get from Kyiv to Ivano-Frankivsk by a fast train. An evacuation train took even longer.

People were sitting on the floor, squeezing into every corner they could. Still, after spending a few nights in the subway, hiding from bombs, Yasia and Sashko were used to that – just as they were to the endless crying of babies. The never-ending noise was wrecking their nerves. They wanted to run away, but there wasn't anywhere they could run to. At the underground station, there was at least the illusion of privacy, while in the train, even the corridor was crammed with people, and they had to step over their neighbours to get to the toilet.

A pretty young woman with long hair was sitting next to them, holding a toddler on her lap. The little girl was crying without stopping, loudly and angrily. Her mother tried to distract her with a teddy bear, but she just threw it on the floor.

"Dada!" the little girl yelped, trying to wriggle out of her mother's arms.

"Daddy can't come with us, honey," the young woman said, sobbing. "He's burying bad guys in the ground. He'll come back after he buries them all."

Sashko saw Serhiy's face jerk. It looked weird.

"Your husband is…" Kateryna, Yasia's mother, started cautiously, touching the woman's shoulder.

"Defending Kyiv," the woman smiled sadly. "It's hard for our little girl. She doesn't understand why her dad is not with us."

"She'll understand it later," Sashko found himself saying. "She'll

1

UKRAINE
603,700 KM²

grow up and will be proud of him. It's hard when your dad is fighting, but it's much easier when he is defending Ukraine, not ... not the other way round."

He barely squeezed the last few words out. He wanted to fall right through the ground or just run away. Yasia kept him still, clutching his hand. She even moved a bit closer, but Sashko was afraid she'd back off once she learned about his father. Yasia drew attention to herself, asking loudly:

"So, how did the war start? In 2014, I mean."

"Well ... you could say **they started to prepare for this war the moment Ukraine proclaimed independence**," Serhiy said warily. "Russia did not want to recognize the right of the neighbouring countries to be free and forced them in every way it could to stay under the powers of its empire ... even if unofficially. 'Why do you need to dub movies in Ukrainian? It's expensive, and you're a small poor country. Here – use the Russian dubbing. And these are books in Russian – take them. Your country is too small and poor to publish books in your language,' they said."

"But we're the second largest country in Europe!" Sashko protested and immediately felt some relief. It was much better to rant and argue with Serhiy than think about Dad's calls and promises. 'My buddies and I are staying in this cottage,' his dad had said. 'It looks so rich. I found a children's bike here, a cool one. I'll give it to you as a gift when we conquer Kyiv. Your mum asked me for money to buy a bike for your birthday. Now you'll get one for free.'

It was better to travel into the unknown on the evacuation train, crammed full, than get a bike at a cost like that, from the hands of a father like that.

Serhiy laughed out loud.

"You and your friends know it. You know that we're a large country and far from poor. We can handle it. But my generation heard those lies from every iron, as they say, and we believed them without thinking. Some people did think about it, though. And they fought. For books and movies in Ukrainian. For keyboards with the Ukrainian layout. For trading with other countries directly, without Russia as a go-between. For the right to do things as we like it, without waiting for Moscow's permission. Moscow, in its turn, was trying hard to make sure that we had nothing and depended on its kindness.

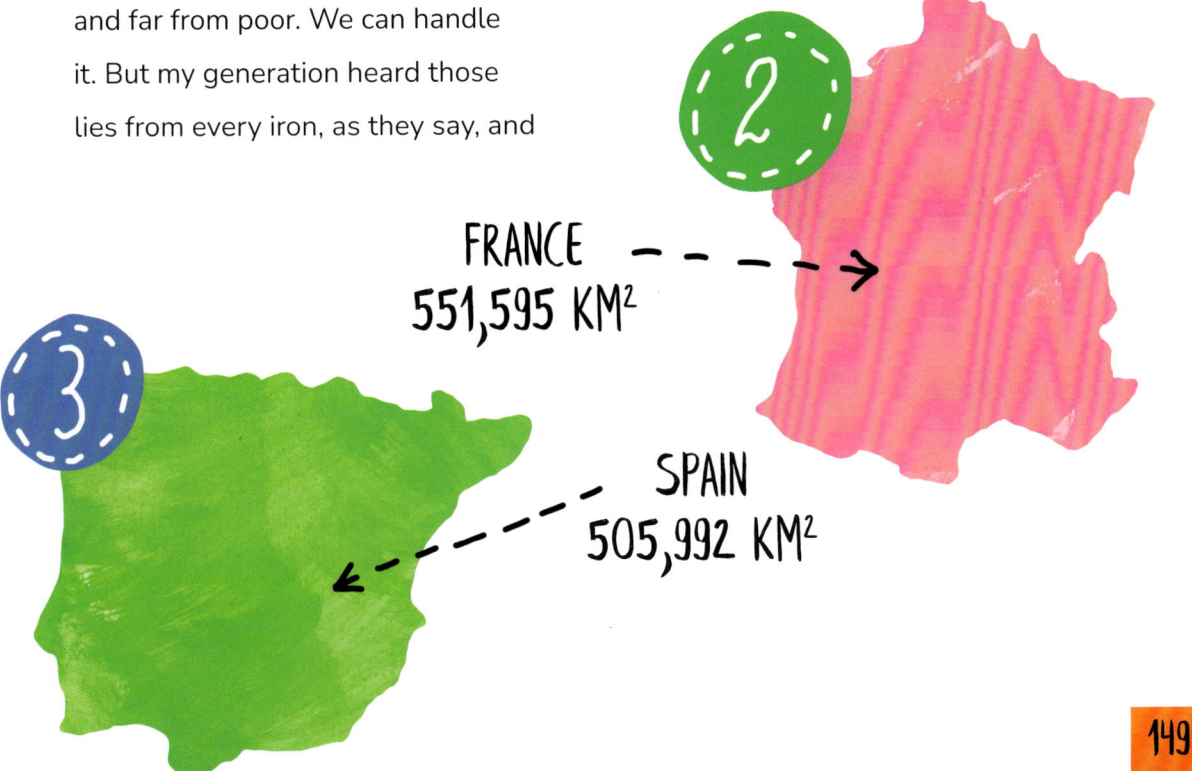

2

FRANCE
551,595 KM²

3

SPAIN
505,992 KM²

"When the revolution of 2013 started, Russia must have realized that its catch was slipping away and tried to conquer Ukraine. It wasn't the first attempt – they had almost gained control of Crimea in 1994 (At that point, Russia tried to occupy Crimea with the help of the mafia. There were also many supporters of Russia in the parliament of the Autonomous Republic of Crimea. But Ukrainian security services pitted the mafia gangs against each other, so they were fighting one another instead of helping Russia but Ukraine spoiled the game back then). So, they spent four years preparing the second attempt."

"Four years?" Kateryna asked incredulously. "You mean even after Yanukovych, their protégé, became president?"

Serhiy nodded.

"That's when they started," he said. "And **in the autumn of 2013, they brought tanks to the Crimean peninsula, violating the agreement**."

"What kind of agreement?" Yasia asked, staring at him.

"They wanted to keep a naval base for their fleet in Sevastopol, and Ukraine didn't have enough power at the time to kick them away. So, they signed an agreement, laying down the conditions for 'renting' the Sevastopol base from us for another twenty-five years. According to it, they were supposed to keep only a certain number of troops there, a limited number of artillery units and no tanks at all. But they broke the deal in September 2013, even before the revolution."

"So, you could say that the revolution saved us," Kateryna said thoughtfully. "They would've attacked us anyway, if they'd been preparing for it since 2010."

Serhiy nodded again.

"But for Crimea, it was already too late. **On 27 February 2014, Russian soldiers occupied**

2014

2013

AUTONOMOUS REPUBLIC OF CRIMEA

the Verkhovna Rada of the Autonomous Republic of Crimea. The Ukrainian military were blocked in their barracks. The peninsula was cut off from the rest of Ukraine."

"What about us?" Sashko asked and broke off. After a pause, he added: "What was Ukraine doing at the time? Did it try to liberate Crimea?"

Yasia's mother sighed.

"Not really. The neighbouring countries and our own citizens — or, rather, Russian agents — yelled that it could not be settled by bloodshed, that people in Crimea wanted to be part of Russia, and that we had no right to stand in their way…"

"Aliye's family didn't want to be part of Russia!" Yasia protested. "And none of the Crimean Tatars did! And who, if not them, had the right to decide on Crimea's destiny?"

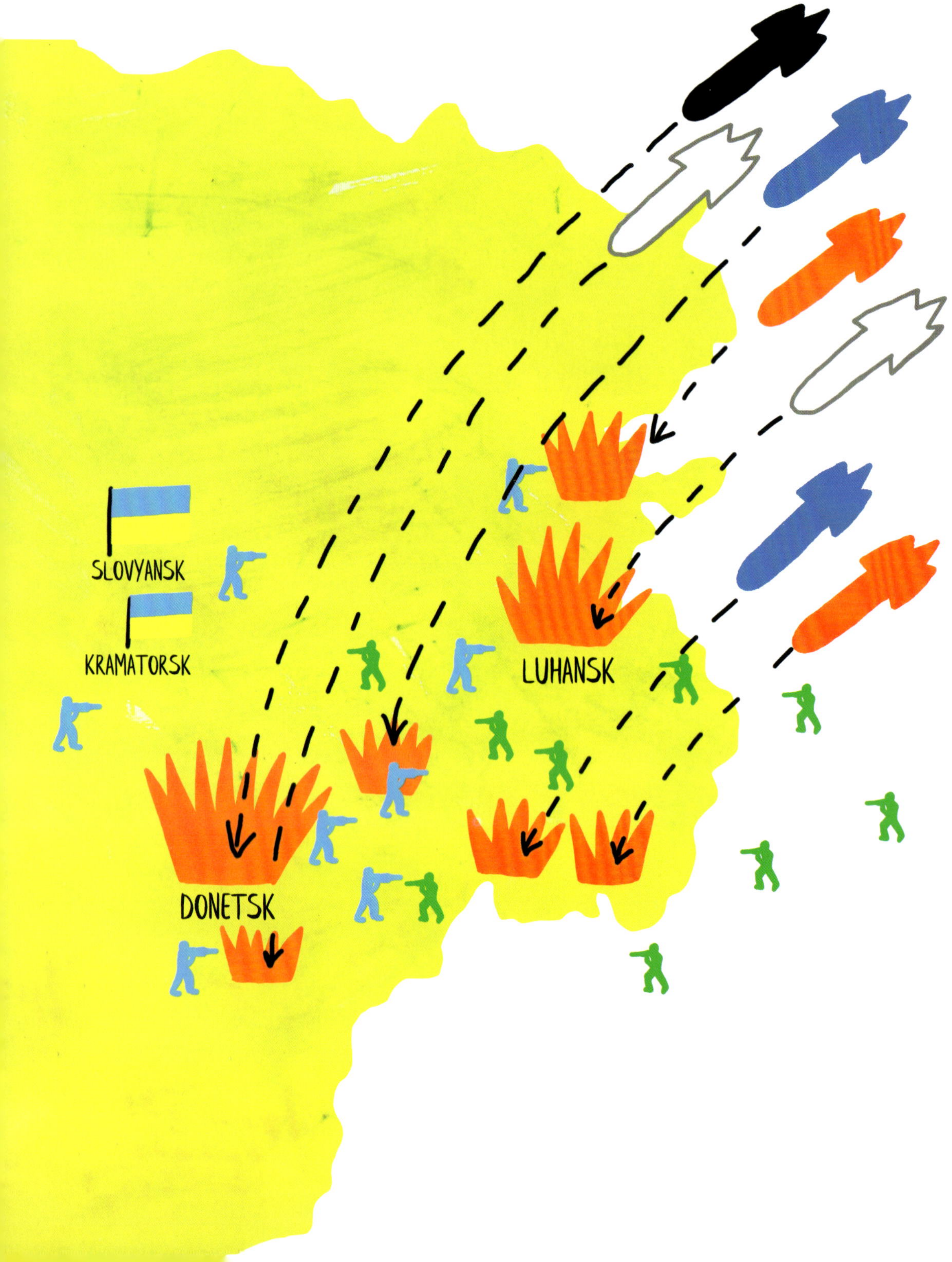
SLOVYANSK
KRAMATORSK
LUHANSK
DONETSK

"Now we know that, dear. But at that moment, we were scared and confused and couldn't believe it was really happening. So, we did nothing. We only withdrew our army from Crimea. Our sailors protested, too, but the Russians blocked their ships in Donuzlav Bay."

"In fact," Serhiy spoke up again, "we did try to liberate Crimea."

Three pairs of children's eyes looked at him with fervent hope in their eyes.

"But those attempts failed, because we were confused and scared – it's true. When the General Staff gave the order to down Russian military jets, this command was not fulfilled. General Voronchenko was organizing the breakthrough of marine corps from Crimea to join the Ukrainian army and lift the blockade of the peninsula, but Russians kidnapped him and disrupted the operation. Under those conditions, even the smallest detail could make the best plan fail. After its success in Crimea, Russia attacked the south and the east of Ukraine. And I don't think they would've stopped had they succeeded there."

"So how did we hold out?" Oksana asked, and Yasia looked at her sister with gratitude. She herself didn't dare to ask about it.

Serhiy smiled.

"It was a miracle, kids. But not only that: we were also holding on to each other and to Ukraine.

"Russia tried to stage a show for the world. It pretended that it was not occupying Ukrainian regions, but it was rather the locals who wanted their villages and towns to go over to Russia. Groups of militants claimed they were ordinary people living in the regions who were 'willing' to join Russia. It also turned out that the local government was teeming with enemy agents.

"In the end, the Ukrainian

government coped with most provocations, so Russia managed to gain a foothold only in the Donetsk and Luhansk regions in April 2014. There were lots of battles worth writing books about. Russian mercenaries who pretended to be locals occupied towns, while Russian artillery was firing at our soldiers from behind the Ukrainian–Russian border…

"But we didn't give up. The Ukrainian army was trying hard to break the enemy formations down into smaller parts, dividing and conquering them. **The liberations of Slovyansk and Kramatorsk were, probably, the biggest successes**, since those operations were just perfect, almost bloodless. The same strategy was supposed to be used in Donetsk…"

An air raid siren went off on Kateryna's smartphone. Yasia and Oksana jumped to their feet. Their mother quickly turned it off and calmed them down.

"Sorry, it's in Kyiv," she said. "I forgot to change the app settings."

Yasia breathed out heavily and plopped down on the floor, putting her head in her sister's lap. In Kyiv, they were hiding from bombs in the subway. In Chernihiv, there was no subway, and one day, on their way down to the basement, they saw a missile hitting a building. After that incident, her father insisted that her mother took her and her sister out of town.

"Air raid sirens blare almost all

CYBORG

day long in Kyiv … Why didn't we have them in the previous years, I wonder?"

Her mother thought for a moment.

"Well, according to the terms of the ceasefire…" She fell silent. "Everyone knew that the ceasefire was supposed to ensure that there would be no attack on Kyiv, no occupation of Kherson and no siege on Chernihiv."

Serhiy snorted.

"No way in hell would they have obeyed the terms of the ceasefire had we not held on to our railway junctions and airfields. They kept staging the show about 'people's militias', but the only jets a people's militia could have would be the ones seized from Ukraine. If Russia had occupied at least one airfield, it would've deployed its jet fighters there and pretended they were trophies captured from Ukraine."

"But our army withdrew from Donetsk airport in the end…"

Kateryna said hesitantly. "I was wondering why they held on to it for so long and did not withdraw earlier. A whopping 242 days…"

"You're right. They withdrew both from Donetsk and Luhansk airports," Serhiy said with a half-smile. "But they did it only after ensuring that no plane would be able to land at either of them."

MINSK AGREEMENTS
5 SEPTEMBER 2014

Sashko stared at his mother's friend. He talked about the airports so proudly, as if he'd been defending them himself.

"But why didn't they liberate Donetsk?" Sashko asked. "Why wasn't my hometown, Makiyivka, liberated?"

Serhiy lowered his head.

"Because the regular Russian troops crossed the border," he said. "We'd been fighting with the saboteurs up until that point and found ourselves not ready for anything like this. Ukrainian soldiers were encircled just outside the small town of Ilovaisk in August 2014. During the negotiations, Russia promised to provide a green corridor to let them leave the area.

"But in fact, the Russians secretly deployed their tanks and artillery and shelled the green corridor as soon as our warriors started to move through it. Over 300 Ukrainian fighters were killed, and Ukraine was forced to sign a ceasefire known as the Minsk Agreements. Our allies

— in particular, France and Germany — promised to be their guarantors."

"Why didn't they help us fight then?" Oksana asked, stroking Yasia's hair.

"They are peaceful European countries. They don't fight."

"Oh, really?" Oksana snickered. "I've recently prepared a report on Northern Africa for my geography class, and I discovered that the United States and France helped Mali crush the Tuareg rebellion. Just a year before the war in Ukraine broke out."

Silence fell.

"But in our case," Kateryna said finally, "they decided it was most important to cease the hostilities at any cost. Even if this cost was our people staying in the occupied territories."

Hearing that, Sashko was about to protest, when Serhiy put his hand on his shoulder. For the first time, the boy didn't feel like shrugging it off.

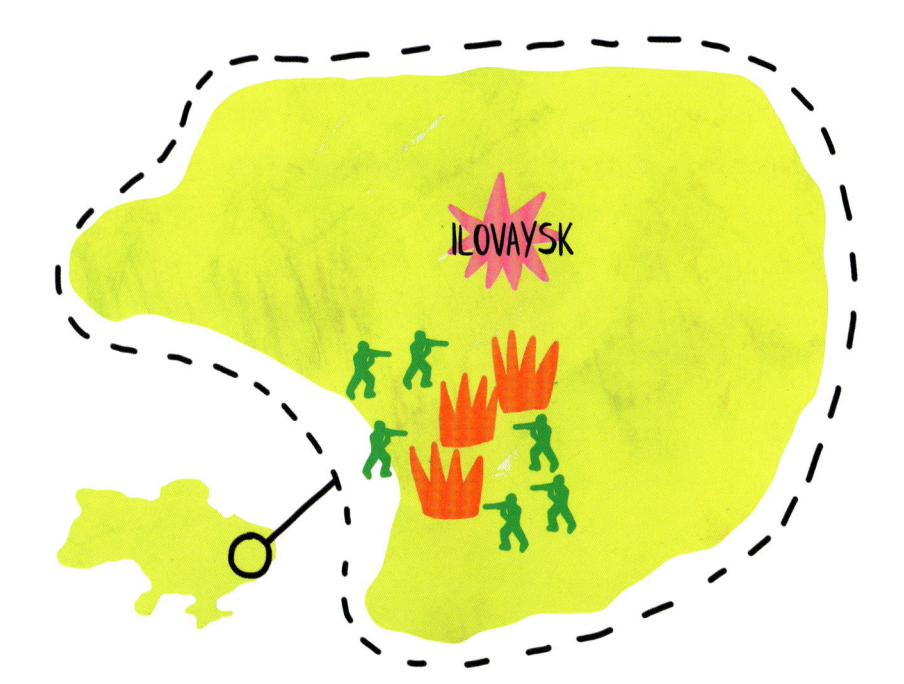

"We've never, ever agreed to forget about our people and our land," Serhiy said. "But we needed some time to find a workable solution to rescue our fellow citizens and liberate the occupied territories. However, Russia violated the Minsk Agreements from day one. Intimidation was the only negotiation strategy the Russians used. And now it looks like they got bored of this 'people's militia' game and launched a full-scale invasion earlier this year."

"So, what will happen now?" Yasia wondered. Closing her eyes, she could see the ruined buildings in Chernihiv. She heard the frightened voice of her mother's friend from Irpin who told them not to go there because Russian troops were already in town, killing people and looting houses. She saw the pale face of Dmytryk, whose mother was fighting on the frontline, defending the region of Luhansk, while he and his father and sister could not leave Odesa, where the Russian paratroopers could've landed any day.

Yasia wished she could see completely different things. But that was what the world around her looked like.

"Now..." Serhiy said stoically, "we have no other choice than to banish them away from our land. From all our land."

"You think it's possible? Can you really defeat such a powerful army?" Yasia asked doubtfully.

After a pause, Serhiy said:

"You know, kids, we just have to do it. If we fail – you'll have to. But I want you to live in peace when you grow up."

His words sounded much more realistic and honest than any assurances that they "would certainly win", so Yasia only nodded gravely.

"Let's get some sleep," her mother said, sighing. "Tomorrow, you'll finally see Aliye."

The children quickly fell asleep. Kateryna opened her vacuum flask, took a sip and asked, staring out of the window:

"Don't you belong to the

operational reserve?" (These are people with combat experience mobilized in case of emergency. In Ukraine, the operational reserve was mobilized on day one of the full-scale Russian invasion.), don't you?" You know all too well how things went in the first year of the war…"

Serhiy nodded and gently ruffled Sashko's hair – the boy was fast asleep.

"I should've been standing in line at the enlistment office ten days ago. But Olha, Sashko's mother, got stuck in the occupied territories, and there was no one else to take care of the boy. I had to take him to a safe place before going back to the army. I hope Ukraine will forgive me."

Kateryna sighed and, turning away from the window, looked him in the eyes:

"Ukraine is fighting for the future of these children. I'm sure it will thank you for what you did."

RUSSIAN AGGRESSION OVER THE

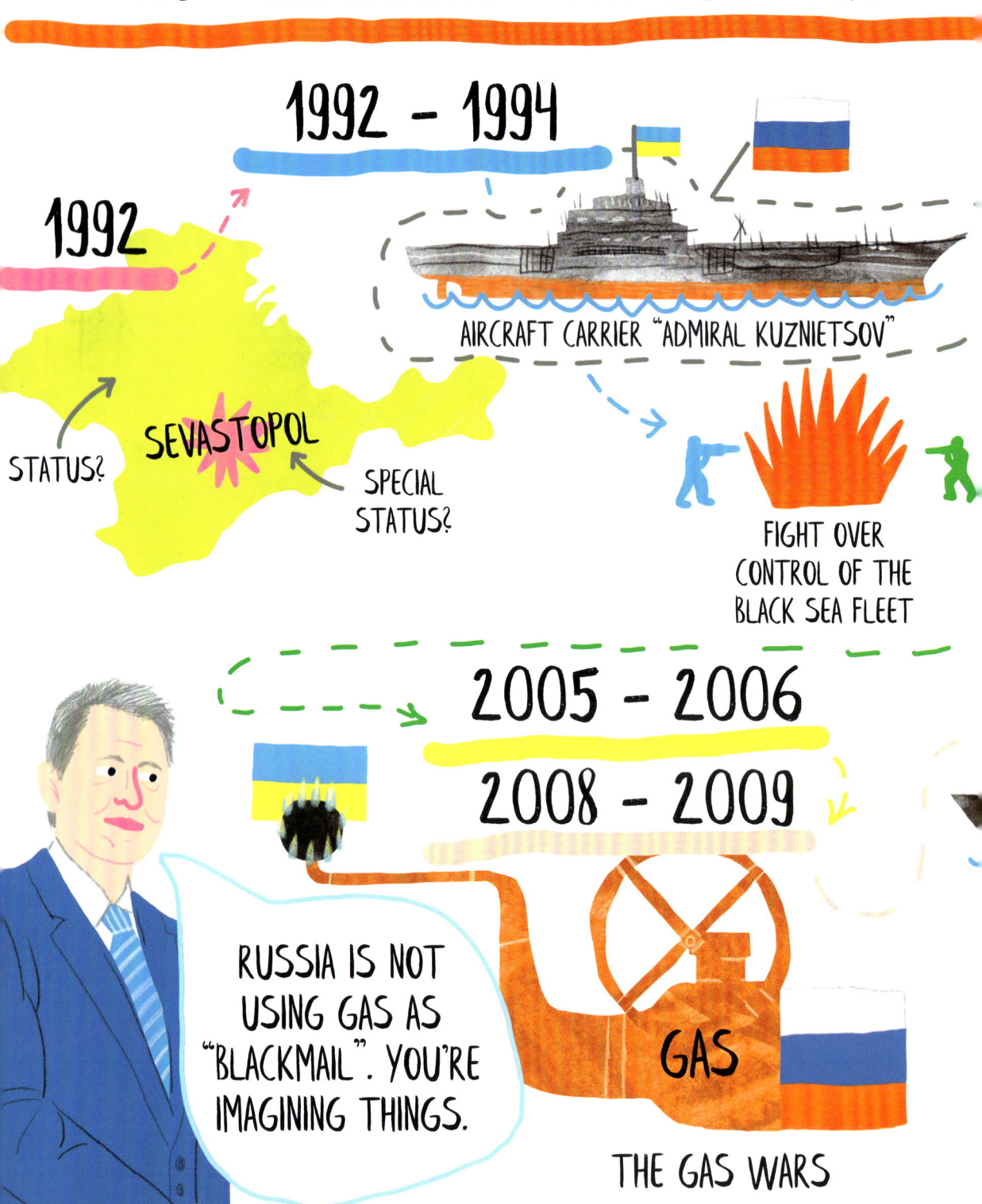

1992 – 1994

1992

STATUS?

SEVASTOPOL

SPECIAL STATUS?

AIRCRAFT CARRIER "ADMIRAL KUZNIETSOV"

FIGHT OVER CONTROL OF THE BLACK SEA FLEET

2005 – 2006
2008 – 2009

"RUSSIA IS NOT USING GAS AS "BLACKMAIL". YOU'RE IMAGINING THINGS."

GAS

THE GAS WARS

YEARS OF UKRAINE'S INDEPENDENCE

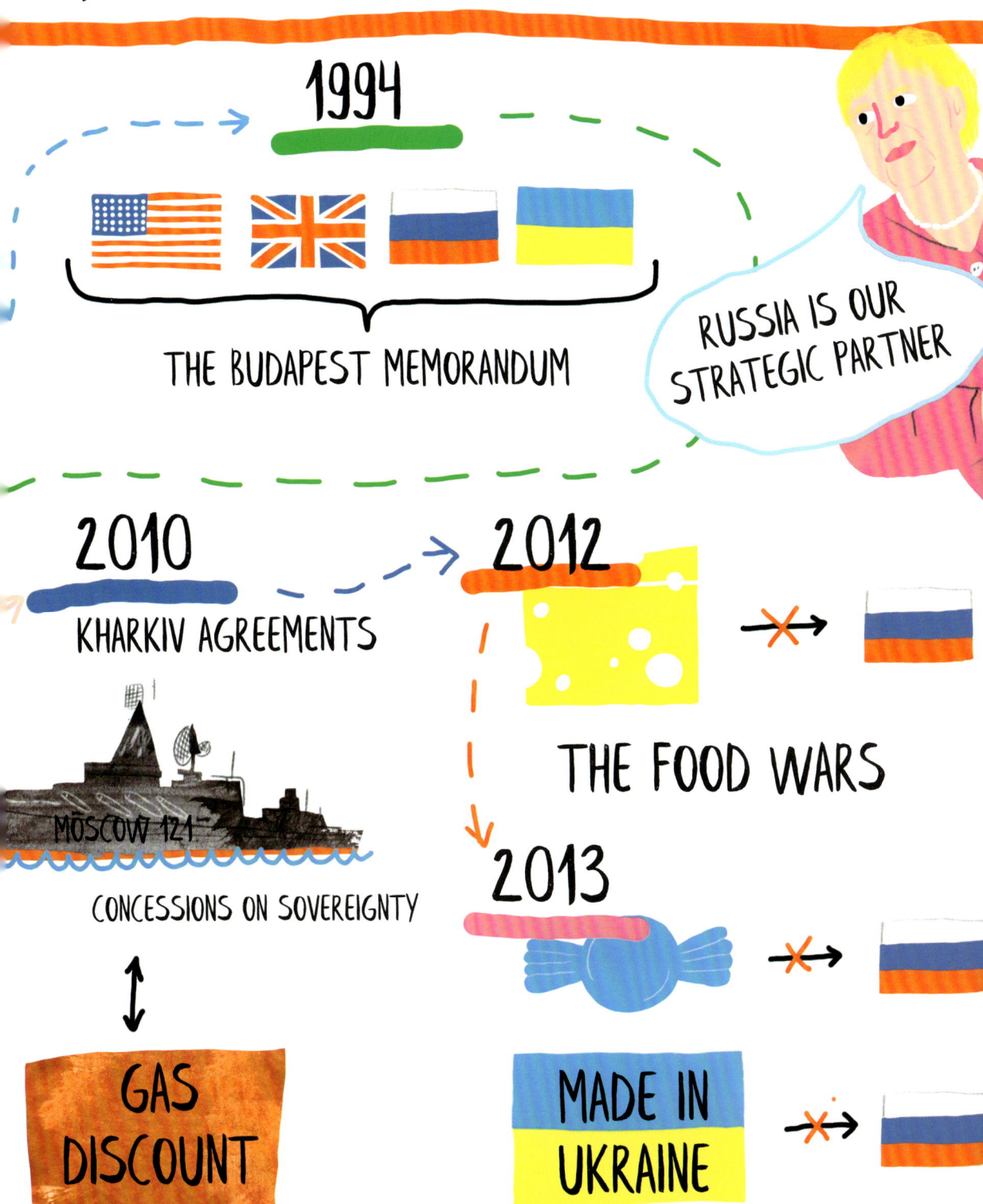

1994

THE BUDAPEST MEMORANDUM

RUSSIA IS OUR STRATEGIC PARTNER

2010

KHARKIV AGREEMENTS

MOSCOW 121

CONCESSIONS ON SOVEREIGNTY ↕ **GAS DISCOUNT**

2012

THE FOOD WARS

2013

MADE IN UKRAINE

14

14 WE ARE NOT SAYING GOODBYE

This book has come to an end, but history does not stop even for a moment. The war in Ukraine continues, and we keep writing and translating new books even under enemy fire.

SEE YOU IN OUR NEXT BOOK!

GLOSSARY

Annexation – Taking over territory from another country by force.

Ally or Allied Powers – Countries formally working together. In WWI and WWII the Allied countries fought against the Axis powers.

Axis – Countries allied with Germany during WWII, including Italy and Japan.

Central Powers – One of the opposing parties during WWI, the Central Powers was an alliance made up of Germany, Austria-Hungary, the Ottoman Empire and Bulgaria.

Climate – The average weather conditions found in a particular place over a long time.

Communism – A type of government, where everything is owned by the whole society and wealth is shared equally by everyone.

Concentration camp – A prison where people are unlawfully held for political reasons, such as being members of a particular group.

Continent – A large mass of land. Earth has seven continents.

Coup – A sudden and usually violent attempt to seize power from an existing government.

Dinosaur – Prehistoric reptiles that existed on Earth about 200 million years ago. Although dinosaur are now extinct, birds are a type of dinosaurs that still exist.

DNA – The common name for deoxyribonucleic acid, DNA is the genetic information stored inside the cells of living things.

Dynasty – A series of rulers from successive generations of one family.

Ecosystem – All the living and non-living things in a particular area. Deserts, rainforest, savannah, grassland and tundra are examples of different ecosystems.

Empire – A collection of lands and territories led by one ruler or government.

Epidemic – An outbreak of a disease that spreads quickly and infects lots of people.

Famine – A long-term shortage of food that can cause starvation and death.

First World War – Taking place between 1914–1918, this was a global conflict that was fought in Europe and involved many countries around the world, including countries in Africa, Asia and the Middle East.

Fossil – The remains of plants and animals that usually lived millions of years ago and eventually turned to rock. Many fossils are made from dinosaur remains.

Glacier – A thick body of ice that covers a large area of land.

Genes – The parts of cells that determine what traits are inherited from your parents, such as height and hair or eye colour.

Genocide – The deliberate killing of a large number of people that belong to a certain religious, ethnic or political group.

Genus – A classification of species that includes lots of living things that are closely related. For example, the genus Canis includes all species of dogs, such as wolves, jackals, dingoes and coyotes.

Gondwana – The name of one of the two supercontinents that was created when Pangea split apart over 200 million years ago.

Herbivore – A type of animal that only eats plants.

Ice age – A period of Earth's history, when the climate became extremely cold, and large areas of the Earth's surface were covered in ice. Ice ages can last for millions of years.

Kasha – A dish commonly prepared in Eastern European countries, it is usually made with buckwheat but can also be cooked with a wide variety of grains, such as oats, wheat, rice and many others.

Khaganate – Sometimes known as a khanate, this was a state or territory ruled over by a king known as a "khan".

Kingdom – A country ruled over by a king or queen.

Laurasia – An ancient supercontinent, this was one of the continents that formed when Pangea split up.

Mammals – Warm-blooded creatures that have backbones and hair. Female mammals, such as elephants, nourish their young with milk produced from mammary glands.

Metallurgy – The study of metals or the process of making things from metals.

Meteorite – A rock or chunk of metal that falls from space to land on Earth.

Migration – Movement of animals from one area of the world to another. Many animal species migrate to leave harsh living conditions, such as drought, winter or food shortages.

Mollusc – A group of animals with soft bodies and no backbones, such as octopuses and snails. Many molluscs have shells.

Native – A person, animal or plant that was born in, grew in, or whose family comes from a particular place.

Neolithic Revolution – A time period referring to when people began to move away from a nomadic lifestyle and hunting practices and formed permanent settlements, cultivated plants and bred animals for food.

Nomad – A person who moves from place to place, maybe in search of food or people to trade with, and doesn't settle down anywhere.

Pangea – A global supercontinent that existed millions of years ago before breaking apart to form smaller continents. Most of the land found on Earth was found in Pangea.

Pogrom – An organized attack or murder of an ethnic group, such as Jews.

Predator – An animal that hunts and eats other animals.

Prey – A creature that is a source of food for other animals.

Principality – A small area of land that is ruled over by a prince.

Reptiles – A cold-blooded animal that relies on external heat sources to regulate its body temperature. Reptiles have scales or bony plates instead of hair or feathers and most reproduce by laying eggs. Crocodiles, snakes and lizards are all types of reptiles.

Second World War – A global conflict between two groups of countries, the Allies and the Axis. The main Allied powers were Great Britain, the Soviet Union, the USA, China and France. The Axis was made up primarily of Germany, Italy and Japan.

Serfdom – A type of forced labour, where the serf (labourer) worked a particular person's land and could not leave without their permission. If the land was sold, the serf was sold with it.

Species – A group of living things who are all very similar and capable of producing offspring, such as lions.

Tribe – A group of people who live together and share the same language, culture or ancestors.

Tsar – A Russian title for an emperor or ruler. A female ruler is called a tsarina.

Tundra – A large area of land with no trees.

Inna Kovalyshena was born in the village of Mankivtsi in Podillia, a region that has seen many important twists and turns in Ukraine's history. Perhaps this is what motivated her to train as a history teacher. She has dreamed of becoming a writer ever since she was a little girl. Before this dream finally came true, Inna had worked as a teacher, a scriptwriter in the film and game industry, and a journalist at a fantasy zine. Her first book – the one you're holding in your hands now – was published two months before Russia's full-scale invasion of Ukraine, and the epilogue was written amid the war in between the air raid sirens.

Galochka Ch is an illustrator and lecturer based in Lviv, Ukraine. Holding a master's degree in graphic design, she is a prolific illustrator and an active participant in professional exhibitions and contests. She also teaches at the Lviv National Academy of Art. Halyna was twice shortlisted for Ukrainian Design: The Very Best Of. Since the war in Ukraine started, she has been involved in several charity projects and exhibitions and launched her own project – drawing classes for adults – where people draw together in a supportive and safe environment.

INDEX

air raid sirens 154–5, 175
Algirdas (Lithuanian grand duke) 70–2
ammonites 11–13, 16
artillery 150, 154, 156
artists 24, 98, 110, 129, 175
Austria 62, 92, 94, 96, 98, 105, 107

Bandera, Stepan (Ukrainian nationalist) 121, 123–4
battles 60, 74, 140, 154
Belarus 70, 72
belemnites 10–11, 13
Black Sea 14–15, 38, 75, 136–7, 160
Bolsheviks 106–10, 116–17, 121
Bronze Age 28, 33
Byzantium (Constantinople) 46–50

Carpathians 12, 28–9, 118, 120, 122
cathedrals 50–1
ceasefires 155–8
Christians 48, 72, 81–3, 86
churches 51, 83
civil wars 69–70, 86, 107
communists 107–8, 121, 124, 130, 168
Cossacks 79, 81–4, 86, 93–4, 96, 99, 132
Crimea 9, 12, 34, 38, 45, 66–75, 78–86, 93–4, 106, 116, 125, 130, 133, 136–43, 150–3

dinosaurs 9–10, 12–13, 15
Dnipro River 38, 46–7, 82
Donbas 12, 29
Donetsk 152, 154–6

empires 34–5, 39, 45, 47–50, 57–8, 80–2, 86, 92–4, 96–9, 104–6, 108, 110, 132, 148, 169
exiles 67, 69, 75, 98, 110, 125, 133, 142

feudalism 57, 60, 96
First World War 105, 109, 118, 169
fossils 9, 11, 15

Gediminas (Lithuanian grand duke) 70–2
genocide 117–18, 169
Germany 94, 107–8, 118, 120–1, 157, 172

Golden Horde 69–70, 73–5
Greeks 33–6, 38–9, 47–8, 58

Hacı Giray (Crimean khan) 75
Herodotus (Greek historian) 33–4, 36
Hetmanate 78, 86–7, 93–5, 97
Homo sapiens 16–17, 22–4
Hungary 58, 62, 105, 107–8, 120, 122
hunger 116–17, 132

ice ages 8, 15, 25
independence 1, 42, 67, 75, 84, 93, 97, 102, 105–6, 110, 114, 121–4, 129–30, 133, 136, 139–40, 143, 148, 160–1

Janike Khanım Tomb 74–5
Jews 86–7, 118, 121, 171
Jurassic period 11–12

Kazakhstan 98, 102–3
khanate 67, 69, 75, 80–2, 84, 86, 93–4, 170
Kotliarevsky, Ivan (Ukrainian poet) 96–7
Kyiv 46–51, 57–9, 62–3, 70, 73, 87, 92, 96, 99, 106, 108–9, 132–3, 136, 139, 146–7, 149, 154–5

Lithuania 62, 72–5, 80–1, 83–4, 86, 94
Luhansk 15, 152, 154–5, 158
Lukianenko, Levko (Ukrainian nationalist) 130, 133
Lviv 60, 92, 109, 121, 124, 132, 175

Makiyivka 32–3, 90–1, 129, 142, 156
Mamay (Crimean general) 69, 72
mammoths 14–16, 24–5
March of the Defenders 139–40, 143
Mongols 58, 60–2, 70
Muscovy 80, 93
museums 21, 25–6, 51

nationalists 118–19, 121–2
Nazis 118, 121–2, 124–5
Neanderthals 22–4
Neolithic Revolution 25–6
nomads 28, 34, 38, 58, 61, 171

Odesa 123, 137–8, 158
Ottomans 80–2, 86, 93–4

parliaments 106, 132, 150
peasants 57, 59, 81, 84, 86, 96, 99, 116–17
Podillia 28, 175

poets 98, 110, 129, 131
Poland 58, 62, 70, 80–4, 86, 93–4, 108–10, 117–18, 122
political parties 105, 118, 130, 132–3, 138–9
Polovtsians 44, 60–1, 70

revolutions 84, 86–7, 105–6, 121–2, 132, 138–42, 150
Romans 39, 45, 47
Rus 48–9, 54, 57–8, 61–2, 70, 72, 80, 96
Russians 90, 93–6, 99, 102, 104–10, 114, 116, 128–32, 136–41, 148–61, 175

Sarmatians 38–9, 44
Scythians 34–9, 44, 132
Second World War 120–1, 123
serfdom 96, 98–9, 172
Sevastopol 150, 160
Shevchenko, Taras (Ukrainian poet) 97–8, 102, 136–7
slavery 36, 81, 96, 99
Soviet Union 116–18, 120–2, 124–5, 129–32, 136, 138, 172
steppes 16, 25, 29, 35, 130, 142, 8175
students 118, 132

Tatars 9, 45, 67, 70, 72, 75, 78–9, 81, 133, 136–7, 141, 151
Tokhtamysh (Crimean ruler) 72, 74
trade 26, 35–6, 38–9, 46–8, 57–8, 81, 149, 171
Trypillyans 26–8
Turkestan 102–3

Ukrainian language 81, 97, 105, 110, 129, 138–9, 148–9, 164
Ukrainian Sich Riflemen 104–6, 118, 122
underground networks 121, 130, 133

Wild Fields 80–1, 94
women 8, 33, 36, 38–9, 42–5, 67, 102, 106, 137, 139, 141, 143, 158–9

Yanukovych, Viktor (Ukrainian prime minister) 138–40
Yushchenko, Viktor (Ukrainian prime minister) 138–9

Zaporizhzhia Sich 82–3, 93–4, 97